Amazing Credit Repair

Boost Your Credit Score, Use Loopholes (Section 609), and Overcome Credit Card Debt Forever

The trademarks that are used are without any consent, and the publication of the trademark is without permission or backing by the trademark owner. All trademarks and brands within this book are for clarifying purposes only and are the owned by the owners themselves, not affiliated with this document.

Published by Newstone Publishing

ISBN 978-1-989726-10-5 (paperback)

Table of Contents

14

Introduction

Your credit rating is important to your daily life. You need to have a good credit rating if you want to ensure you can get access to the financial services that you desire. You must also have a good rating to ensure you can handle the best possible rates on whatever you are interested in utilizing.

But at the same time, it only takes a moment for your credit rating to be put at risk of harm. Your rating might be damaged due to many things like missing credit payments, court-related issues, or anything else that might keep you from getting the money that you need.

Even worse, not having a good credit rating can prove to be dangerous for your financial needs. You might be refused the opportunity to get an auto or mortgage loan. You could even be rejected for a new job due to your credit rating. While you might still be able to qualify for some things, you might struggle to get access to them all due to the added charges you are bearing with due to higher rates over a poor credit rating.

What's more, you might have lots of credit card debts and other expenses that you are struggling to pay down. People who have poor credit ratings are often those who have large amounts of expenses. These include many credit card debts that can add up over time. Having too many debts will cause you to lose credit rating points. Even worse, you may end up in a situation where you are living from one paycheck to the next, not to mention your inability to cover an emergency without adding more debts than what you need.

The problems that come with not having a good credit rating can be dangerous. However, you do not have to worry about having a poor rating for too long provided that you use the right efforts for getting the best credit rating you can possibly earn.

This guide will help you with identifying what you can do to get a better credit rating for your life. You will read here about many things relating to your credit including what goes into your rating. You can figure out what you can do to improve upon your credit rating based on what can go into that rating and how it can make a real difference in your life.

You will also see what you can do for your credit repair needs through this guide. You may find that it is not hard for you to restore your credit in the event you have been harmed by something in the past.

Much of this guide helps you with understanding how you can cover the expenses associated with your credit cards. You can work to pay off all those debts while also managing your cards well in the future.

In fact, you might be surprised at how intricate and detailed the world of credit cards can be. You will see throughout this guide that there are many ways how your credit cards are laid out and that many terms go into them. Knowing what you are getting out of your cards and how they work is critical to your success regarding being able to cover those cards and to keep them from costing more to utilize than what you can afford.

The details on what you can do for managing your credit are varied. You can use many sensible strategies for managing your credit while using the right decisions. You can also get in touch with credit reporting bureaus to get any problems you have on your report fixed up.

There are even various intriguing loopholes and secrets relating to your credit that you can utilize. Many of these entail some of the various laws that can be utilized to help you grow your credit and manage any of the errors that might have come about on your report. This includes working to reverse any of the decisions that might have been made against you when it comes to your credit history. You can use these to help yourself with improving upon your credit and getting the most out of your work.

The best part is that all of these details are ones that you can utilize yourself. You might not have to spend more money than what you are trying to cover on your credit profile. That is, you don't have to contact some outside credit repair group that would not do much of anything to help you. More importantly, you will not have to worry about such a credit repair group ripping you off with the false belief that you could get some real credit help from that entity.

Of course, sometimes you might be working well on managing your credit but it could suddenly take a massive hit if your identity is stolen. This guide also includes details on how you can repair your credit rating in the event you are a victim of identity theft. This is a legitimate problem that has become more commonplace throughout the world, so it is critical for you to see what you can do to resolve your credit-related issues following a case where you have been victimized by identity theft.

The details you will come across in this guide will assist you with resolving the many problems you might come across when it comes to your credit rating. Be sure to see what this guide has to offer so you can find that it is not overly hard for you to get the most out of your work with improving upon your credit.

Notice

The information in this credit repair guide primarily concentrates on credit repair ideas and concepts that may be used in the United States. Although many of the concepts introduced here can be utilized throughout the entire world, the data listed here focuses mainly on legal ideas for American use.

The concepts introduced here are for helping people to manage their credit needs, but it was not necessarily produced with a specific type of situation or entity in mind. The producers of this guide cannot guarantee that you will experience positive results off of your credit repair efforts. Your success will vary based on your individual situation. Using the points in this guide may help anyone with managing their funds.

The information in this guide is accurate as of July 2018. There is a potential for some standards from FICO surrounding your credit score to change.

Some of the points listed in this guide also entail legal actions that involve going into a court. Although these are optional actions to consider, they are still options that may work and therefore would entail significant risks. Be aware of the risks you are entering into when getting into any legal actions associated with your credit repair needs.

Chapter 1 – What Makes Your Credit Score What It Is?

Your credit score is vital to your life. It is something that helps you to enjoy life as you have added access to financial services and various investments. You must understand how your score can directly influence what you can purchase so that you can enjoy your life.

The problems you have with your credit score can be very dramatic and you might not be fully aware of what affects your credit score or how valuable it is to you.

Those people who pay off their debts and lines of credit with on-time payments will be more likely to have better credit ratings. There are many things relating to your credit score that should be explored that go well beyond just your payment history.

Understanding the Concept of the Credit Score

The idea of the credit score was introduced in 1989 by the Fair, Isaac and Company organization or FICO.

FICO developed the credit score idea to analyze a person's financial history and fiscal health. This was used mainly to help businesses identify the ability of consumers to handle certain financial functions.

The credit data on a person is gathered from major credit bureaus. In the United States, those three bureaus are Equifax, TransUnion, and Experian.

The main intention of the credit score is to help financial service providers and lenders to identify consumers' behaviors before doing business with them. These businesses depend on their customers' ability to repay loans. It is through the credit score one has that it becomes easier for a creditor to decide what can be done for a certain customer.

The credit score is also designed to provide an extensive portrait of someone's credit based on how well that person has been able to manage debts. The score can go back several years. It helps give businesses and others information about whether or not a person is capable of managing debts. Sometimes a person might have just one very minor issue with payments over the course of a few years. That person is not going to be considered a risky individual. In some cases, a person might have multiple debts that make their responsibilities greater and might be extremely hard to pay off and make additional debts risky. It is important to be aware of what might be identified in a report when applying for a loan or an extension of an existing loan.

How Often Is Your Score Updated?

Your credit score will be regularly updated throughout the year. Every major payment you make, every judgment against you, and every inquiry by a financial institution or business will be counted. This makes it all the more important for you to see what your score is.

You have the option to ask for a credit report at any time so you can get regular information on how your credit is being managed. The report you acquire should give you details on everything surrounding your credit and to notice if there are errors that need to be corrected so that your credit score is stronger and more useful.

Chapter 2 – The Parts of Your Credit Score

There are five main parts of a credit score. They are designed to create a more comprehensive setup for your expenses and financial responsibilities.

These five points are listed in order from the most important to least important based on what directly influences your credit score.

Note: The details in this chapter are based on what FICO considers to be the most important. The percentages next to each part are approximate variables that FICO has listed in the past. The group is very secretive as to what it will specifically consider when computing your credit history.

Payment History – 35%

Your payment history refers to how well you are making the payments that you owe on debts and that you are handling them responsibly. In particular, you will need to make your regular payments on-time and in full to keep your credit history healthy.

FICO states that a strong payment history is based on someone's ability to pay debts regularly and to avoid being overextended. Your debts should be easily covered by your income. FICO may not penalize someone heavily for one or two missed payments, but they will review how you made those payments over time. It will become a significant problem for those who cannot handle their finances and miss or are late making payments.

The key for your credit score is to get as many on-time payments as possible. Those who can show they can pay off their debts on-time will receive higher scores.

What Types of Debts Are Factored?

There are many types of debts:

1. Credit cards

You have to pay credit card transactions regularly and on-time as these debts are considered unsecured debts.

All types of credit cards are considered part of your credit history. This includes not only the cards you regularly use but also the ones that you don't use. Those unused cards are seen as open lines of credit that show you have more money to work with at any time.

2. Retail accounts

Any charge card accounts or other accounts with specific retailers will influence your payment history. These accounts are devoted to only one retailer. Although many retailers offer these credit accounts to give customers special benefits and rewards, they will also charge high rates and fees to those who do not pay their debts on-time. The cards from retailers might seem appealing because they offer certain rewards but be careful to pay them off monthly so as not to incur high monthly interest rates.

3. Loans or other long-term debts

These include student loans, car loans, and mortgage loans. You have to make sure those loans are paid off regularly to avoid high interest charges. Your payment history will include details on how well you can pay off those loans.

FICO particularly places an emphasis on mortgage loans. These are high-value loans that have long amortization and have collateral attached to most of those loans. These include vehicles and other items you might have acquired through a loan. Defaulting on a loan and forfeiting your collateral will hurt your credit rating severely.

4. Regular accounts with financial companies

You must watch for how those regular accounts can affect your payment history. You must also make sure they are paid off regularly.

What Happens When You Miss a Payment?

FICO is not necessarily going to penalize you for every single missed payment you might have on your report. FICO will judge you based on many factors relating to that missed payment. This could impact how you are able to handle the payments.

1. How late you are

FICO will penalize you if you are significantly late on your payment. You might not be penalized if you are one or two days late, but the penalty can be significant if you are late one week or more. FICO respects those who are responsible.

2. How much money you owed

You could be penalized more if you owed hundreds or thousands of dollars. A missed payment is then significant.

3. How recent were your missed payments

The impact of a missed payment will be minimal if it was recent and does not constitute a pattern of missed or late payments. Your credit score will improve because it will be noticed that you are responsible with your payments. One missed payment will be a thing of the past after you get back to your regular payment schedule.

4. The number of missed payments

It is one thing to have one missed payment in a year. It is another when you have several of them in a short period of time and, in that case, you will be.

5. Whether or not a debt has been written off

Your credit rating will be hurt dramatically if your creditor determines that you are not going to pay and have written off the debt. In addition, a creditor might not allow you to pay off that charge-off or even have access to the fund account that needs to be covered.

What You Owe – 30%

The second-most important part of your credit history involves the amounts of money that you owe at any given time. Those who spend more money are often reviewed carefully because they are reliant on financial loans.

Six points to understanding what you owe:

1. How much money do you owe on all of your accounts?

The total amount of money that you owe on all your accounts will impact on your credit history. The amount of money listed on each account refers to what you owe on it. A loan payment includes charges for the principal and interest on the loan. For credit and charge cards, the total amount of money that you owe on each of those cards will be listed.

The balance that is listed is generally the one that was shown on your last statement. Therefore, you might have something listed on your credit card even if you already paid a prior month's payment. This suggests that you will have to pay something on the next billing period or else you would have to pay extra interest, which would hurt your overall credit history.

2. What do you owe on certain types of accounts?

The variety of accounts that you have will be a factor. You could be penalized if you owe more money on unsecured debts like charge or credit cards. Anything that entails debts that cannot be retrieved through collateral will make a greater impact on your credit history.

3. How are you using your credit on revolving accounts?

A revolving account refers to an account where you might have a certain amount of money owed in one point versus another. For instance, you might owe $500 on a credit card one month and $70 the next and then $450 after that. This is all based on whatever you have put on that card at a time. Those who pay off their revolving accounts regularly regardless of how much money is added to those accounts will have better credit reports.

One trick that FICO uses involves looking at how much money you are spending on a revolving account when compared with your limit. FICO prefers people who spend well under their limits. For instance, you might have a credit card with a limit of $3,000. Your credit rating will not be hurt if you only spend $600 on that card within a billing period. Meanwhile, your credit rating could be harmed if you spend $2,800.

However, your credit rating might be affected if you do not spend anything against your limit. You have to show that you are capable of working with a limit responsibly.

4. How many accounts do you hold that have balances on them?

The number of accounts you are actively using will influence your credit rating. If you can show that you are responsible for managing many lines of credit at a time without problem, your credit rating will not be affected. If you have lines of credit that have no activity, you could end up being at risk of your credit history being considered unhealthy.

When you have too many accounts with high amounts owed on them, it might indicate that you have overextended your credit and are at risk of serious financial harm.

5. Are you close to maxing out your credit cards or other lines of credit?

This point relates to your ability to use the credit on revolving accounts. While FICO does indeed look at how well you use revolving accounts and that you can pay off varying amounts of them, you must also watch your limits. There's a reason why limits are placed on those cards – the groups that issue the cards don't want to be at risk of people borrowing too much at a time.

Those who are close to maxing out their cards will be damaging their credit score. That is, those people who spend near or at their credit limits will be treated as high-risk borrowers who could be taking in more than what they can afford to manage.

6. What do you owe on a loan when compared with its original amount?

The amount of money you owe on your loan is supposed to go down. Interest charges and other fees may apply, but the principal on your loan should be decreasing. Those who pay on their loans regularly and reduce the totals they owe will have better credit ratings. For instance, a person who borrowed $20,000 for a car loan could have paid $4,000 on it, which amounts to having 80% of the loan still owing. If the loan was repaid in one year by $10,000, then 50% of that loan is still owed. At this point, you are showing that you are indeed paying off your loan as you are supposed to, thus improving upon your credit score.

What if you only paid a few thousand and you had 75% still owing after a year? Your rating will not go up because you are only putting in the minimal effort into handling your loan. Of course, your credit rating will improve if that percentage decreases.

You can only keep that interest on your loan from increasing dramatically if you manage to repay your loans responsibly. This includes making payments above the minimums that you should pay each month.

These six factors will influence your credit score based on how you are repaying debts.

Credit History Length – 15%

FICO appreciates people who are willing to continue using certain credit lines while ensuring those lines is consistently paid off without issues. By showing responsibility with those credit lines, you are indicating you are ready to pay your debts without problems.

People who have larger credit histories are often favored in they might be seen as being able to manage their debts for a long time. At the same time, those people with longer histories might be seen as risky individuals due to how they are continuing to have substantial debts even after many years.

This third part of your credit score is judged on two factors:

1. The average age of each of your accounts

2. The age of whatever the oldest account is

You could benefit if you have covered the same credit card for years and have paid it off consistently over all that time. Creditors appreciate loyalty, and your loyalty could help you to become more appealing and attractive.

Adding new lines of credit is only going to hurt you at this point. By adding a new line, you are just reducing the average length of your cards. This could make you a more high-risk client when all is considered.

There are no golden standards for how long your credit history should be. Your history could last for several years in some cases.

The Types of Credit – 10%

There are many credit choices for you to explore. The key is to simply not open any credit card unless you have a definite plan to use it.

Those who have too many credit accounts might be seen as high-risk borrowers. Therefore, you should look at what you are doing with the accounts you initiate and that you have a sensible plan in hand for how you will manage those accounts.

This is a low-value part of your credit history. You might be encouraged to look at the different types of credit you can take advantage of so you can get something that works well for your financial needs. In the end, it is up to you to decide how to use your credit so it is not hard for you to use and maintain.

Inquiries and New Credit – 10%

The last 10% of your account is dedicated to the inquiries you make. An inquiry takes place when someone looks at your credit account.

Perhaps you wish to apply for a charge card at your favorite local retailer. You would have to consent to that retailer doing a search on your credit history to ensure you can be approved for the card. The search would also determine the credit limit you will have on that card. The retailer would make an inquiry on your credit. At this point, you would be listed as having asked for an inquiry on your credit report.

It is fine and normal to have one inquiry every once in a while. This is especially the case when you are performing your regular credit check with each of the main reporting bureaus.

You could come across some problems if you make too many inquiries within a short period of time. Your credit rating may be hurt when you have lots of inquiries because you are showing an interest in various types of credit options. You will be perceived as a credit risk because you are indicating that you are attempting to increase your debt.

How Far Back Will the Content Go?

The greatest thing about your credit report is that these five points will go back several years. You may find items on your report that are at least seven years old. The credit reports you have are based on how well you have been able to manage money over the years. You must be careful when managing your credit as every mistake you make is going to be on that report for a while.

The content can go back to ten years in the event of a bankruptcy as well. In fact, any serious problems that show up on your report will be reflected on your credit rating. It is one thing to miss a payment and that is not necessarily going to hurt your credit rating much or at all. But it is another when you have been subjected to a court ruling that caused you to declare bankruptcy.

You must be aware of what you are doing when it comes to your credit. Be sure you manage your finances including all your credit cards so that your credit score will be affected positively and not negatively.

Chapter 3 – Credit Card Use and Its Impact on Your Credit

Your credit report will be influenced by many things, but it is through your credit card use that your report might be impacted the most. It is vital for credit cards to be managed properly when their revolving natures are considered.

Many people who have significant credit-related issues have such problems because they did not use their credit cards correctly. It is very easy for people to spend above their financial ability to repay have more unsecured debt than what is healthy. A credit card is not like an installment loan where a very specific amount of money has to be paid every month. It is up to you to decide how you are going to use your credit cards.

Your credit rating can be directly influenced by more than just the amount of money you spend on your credit card. Your credit score will be impacted by many points relating to how your credit card is used.

How Often Do You Use Your Card?

You can use your credit card for many purchases. You can use it for paying for purchases online with ease. Websites can save your credit card data so you can use it as desired. You can even use a credit card to pay for something at a vending machine.

The number of times you use your credit card might influence how well your credit rating will develop. Those who use their credit card more will be interpreted by FICO as being high-risk consumers. They are being too reliant on their credit cards, thus making it easier for them to lose control and add more charges to their cards than necessary.

Those who do not use their cards that often will be less likely to get into financial trouble.

Your credit card use is important and you have to think carefully about how often you are going to use your card and that you recognize what you are spending your card on. This includes not only on spur of the moment charges but also expenses that you might attach to your card.

You may send your card information out to a certain billing company to be used for automatic monthly payments for some kind of service. The goal is to keep from having too many of these payments on a card so that you don't lose track of what you are accumulating as debt.

How Much of Your Limit Is Used?

The credit limit on your card can be a few thousand dollars in most cases. You cannot afford to go too close to your limit as that might be a sign that you are spending too much on something or that you are not in control of your spending.

If you max out that card, you are spending more than what you had intended to use. This is a threat that could end up hurting your credit because it shows you are not willing to work inside the limits that were set for your card.

You can get regular updates online about all your spending and all your payments on each card. Checking online helps you to determine how you are using your card.

What About the Number of Cards?

The total number of cards you have can make a difference in your credit rating. Those who have more credit cards are likely to lose control over how they are paying on their cards, thus making it harder for their credit histories to grow in a healthy way.

Each card has certain benefits attached. These include cards that offer specific types of rewards. Some people also prefer to divide their cards based on different reasons for purchases. One card may be used exclusively for gas purchases while another is made for online orders, for instance. While this might be a convenience for some people, there is always the threat that the cards can get out of hand.

Your credit history might be hurt if you have too many cards at a time. Although you might be able to show that you are responsible to pay on all those cards on-time that does not necessarily mean that you are going to make everything work well for you. Having a number of cards could create a sense of disorganization in your life as you struggle to manage all of those cards.

Keeping your card usage in check based on different concepts is important. Be sure to look at your online accounts to see how you are using them. You can review multiple cards at the same time if they have been provided to you by the same bank or other issuing company.

Late Payment Impact

Late payments are damaging to credit profiles. You could be at risk of significant trouble surrounding what you owe. Late payments on any debts that you have are going to negatively influence your credit report. However, a single late payment might not make an impact on your rating.

You might find that having one late payment versus several on-time payments may not influence your credit history. One late payment may be interpreted as an isolated event. The long-term trend must show that the single late payment is an aberration that is not normal. When this appears, the risk of your credit being hurt will be minimal.

Even with that in mind, it is best for you to watch for how well the payments you make are handled. You must watch carefully for how well the payment is handled and that you are in control over what you are doing with each card you have. Missing just one payment is not going to be a problem if you regularly make payments as usual, but you should still watch for what you are doing with your money and that you don't go overboard with regards to not having enough money on hand.

Keeping your late payments under control is critical. Having a calendar or other solution on hand for managing your payment schedules is always useful. You cannot afford to wait until the last minute to make your payments. It can take a few days or hours for a credit card group or other entity to record your payment. This timing could be even greater if you send your payment out by mail instead of online.

What Constitutes a Late Payment?

A payment on a credit card typically is considered late if it has not been made in the last 30 days. During that 30-day period, you would have the opportunity to pay your credit card in full without incurring added interest charges or fees. After the 30-day period, you will be charged a late fee and also lose points off your credit rating. A credit card company expects you to be able to pay what you owe or at least the minimum amount within that 30-day point.

What About Shared Cards?

An interesting part of today's credit score technology is that your name's appearance on different credit cards can make an impact. When you work with credit cards, you are listing yourself as being an authorized user of those cards.

This can be important if you have a card with multiple people named. You might have a card that has your name and your spouse's name or the name of someone else who is close to you. This means that you and that other person are going to have that card listed on your credit reports.

You must look at how your name is listed on different cards. Even if you are just one of many people whose name is listed as an authorized user on a card, you would still have that card listed on your credit report. Therefore, you should keep tabs on each card that you have in your name and that you fully aware of the charges on it.

Does the Credit Card Brand Make a Difference?

You might have various credit cards that are linked to different credit card companies. Visa and MasterCard are the most popular options, but American Express is also popular. Don't forget about the Discover card and various international brands like Diners Club and JCB.

The credit card brand you have is not going to make an impact on your credit score. Paying off an American Express card on-time is worth just as much as if you paid off your Visa card on-time. Although each company has its own terms for using cards and its own level of prestige, they will all contribute the same to your credit rating.

It is the total amount of money that you owe on a card that will make the biggest impact. You could owe a small amount on an American Express card, but that will not make a huge dent in your credit report than if you owed five times as much on a Discover card.

Having an extended variety of cards from different brands is not going to impact your credit score.

Do these different credit card brands have any differences?

The fact is that these credit card brands are methods of payment that rely upon banks and other issuers to back their cards. MasterCard, Visa, and all those other groups are not going to determine the rates, rewards, or other things you can receive. Rather, they will be reliant on what those banks have to offer.

It is true that some of these card brands will operate their own customer service departments to handle disputes or concerns with some of these cards and how they are paid off. Others might offer different types of card products that can be licensed through banks with some cards offering more rewards or access to special functions. In the end, these cards are dictated by the banks and lenders they partner with. The Visa card system is more of a protocol used by retailers for managing payments, for instance. When Visa teams up with a certain lender, that card company will get its cards out to more people. It's up to that lender to do everything else.

Be aware of how well your card is managed and that you understand what features it has.

Chapter 4 – Debts and Loans

While credit cards are important, you must also look at the loans you are working with. Loans are valuable financial investments that people should not ignore when it comes to what they are doing with their money. It is through loans that people can get the most out of anything they want to acquire.

For instance, you might be interested in getting a new car. Maybe you want an upgrade, or perhaps you prefer to buy a new car. You clearly cannot pay the entire amount up front. A new car could cost tens of thousands of dollars. You might not have enough in your savings or checking account.

That is where a loan can come into play. A loan will provide you with the opportunity to cover the costs associated with a high-end expense. However, while this can be helpful for your purchasing needs, it could also hurt your credit rating if you are not cautious.

A loan will require regular installment payments over time. You must look at how well you are managing the debt that you have incurred.

The loan would specify:

1. The term of the loan – the number of monthly payments required to pay off the loan

2. The minimum payment that you must make on your loan each month

3. The interest rate of your loan

Being able to make the required payments on your loan over a fixed period of time is critical. You could also make more payments beyond the minimum to reduce the total amount of interest you owe on your loan.

You have to be aware of how your loan is going to influence your credit rating. Your loan is going to impact your credit rating by:

1. How much you owe on your loan

2. How the value of your loan changed over time

You should be at a steady rate where your loan is being paid off consistently on-time. The principal on your loan, or the amount that is on the loan before interest is added, should be considered as you work toward paying off the loan.

3. Are you ever late on your loan payments? This includes cases where you don't make a payment during a certain period.

4. How much interest is being applied to the loan payments?

The total amount of interest on that loan should decline as you continue to make payments.

There is always the chance that your credit score will decline if you are not careful. Your score may drop if you fail to make payments or if your payments are less than what was agreed on when the loan was signed.

Even more importantly, the value of your loan might be a factor. Those who make too many loans will have lower credit scores for many reasons. They will have lower scores because they are spending more money than what they might be able to afford. They are getting lots of inquiries recorded on their accounts as well.

A person's credit score will drop dramatically if someone is unable to manage all of the loans one holds. It is easy for people to lose track of their loans because they have different interest rates, payment due dates, and schedules.

Those who have loans must be very careful when it comes to how they are paid off and how they can influence one's credit rating. It is vital for anyone who has a loan to ensure that the loan can be covered and that there is a plan to get a loan managed without problems.

Consider the Interest Rate

The most important part of a loan is the interest rate. Those who have a better credit score will be offered better interest rates on their loans. Then again, those with such good scores would likely be approved to get such loans in the first place.

You would have to improve your credit rating to get a better rate on a loan, not to mention the chance to be accepted for a loan. You can also get your rating up to where you may consider refinancing your loan. This is a point about handling loans that will be discussed later in this guide to help you manage your debts.

Chapter 5 – Things That Are Not Included in Your Credit Report

An important thing to consider is to repair your credit rating to improve their credit histories and make them stronger.

The truth is that there are many things that are not going to impact one's credit history or the credit report. The details in this chapter include points that FICO is not going to record when it comes to your credit.

The good news is that many of the things that are not going to be found on your credit report are ones that you don't have any control over. With that in mind, you can at least keep yourself from struggling with issues that you would never be able to resolve. There are many other things that you can do that will improve your credit rating.

Demographics

Your demographics are not going to be a factor. These include details on your age, gender, race, ethnicity, marital status, sexual orientation, and where you live. The goal of not including these details is to ensure that no biases are in play when considering a credit score.

The bureaus do not discriminate against certain people because of particular concerns they might have. The Consumer Credit Protection Act has been added to ensure that these groups will not include your demographic data.

Any information about your demographics can be used for research intentions only. That is, a group may choose to review that data to determine which segments of the population are likely to use certain services. This, in turn, lets a group decide how it will market its services to the public in the future.

Your demographic information will not be listed on your credit report. They will not appear on your account with a financial service provider either. In fact, any demographic details that a group finds will be basic content that cannot be used to directly identify a specific person. Therefore, you should not be worried about your data being used to influence your ability to manage your finances.

Interest Rates

The interest rate is an expense that will cause quite an impact on one's expenses and the ability to pay them off. You have to review your interest rate so you know what you would have to pay off while also having a smart plan to do so.

All credit cards, charge cards, and loans include interest rates among other charges. These interest rates are imposed so that financial institutions are paid for lending money to customers. They do not lend money without receiving payment for their services.

A credit report is not going to be focused on the interest rate of whatever you are using. That is, you should not assume that your credit rating will improve if you handle high-interest funds or investments. The interest rates of your loans will not be found on your report.

Your credit report will only focus on how much money you owe at a given time and how you are paying it off. There is nothing on that report showing the interest rate you are paying off. Therefore, it might help to look for lower rates for loans or charge cards.

Are Income and Employment History Important?

Your ability to earn an income is not going to be a factor in your credit score. That is, you are not going to be hurt because you do not have a job or your line of work is not as steady as it could be. This is vital for freelancers whose pay schedules are irregular or those who were laid off, on disability, or in some other situation that caused a person to become involuntarily unemployed.

The total amount of income you earn is not going to make an impact on your credit score. You do not have to earn a high income to have a good credit rating. It is what you do with your money that makes a difference, not whether or not you earn enough money.

What Types of Inquiries Are Not Considered?

As mentioned earlier, the inquiries on your credit report will influence your credit score slightly. But that does not mean every type of inquiry is going to appear on your report. Many inquiries will be considered minimal.

Some of the inquiries that are not going to impact your credit rating include the following:

- Inquiries made by your employer

- Pre-approved offers that do not reflect official offers for credit

- Any requests you made on your own to review your credit report

- Requests from a lender you are working with; these include requests that a lender uses to determine if you should get a better rate or if you should be promoted to take advantage of certain investments

Keeping the number of inquiries down is helpful regardless of whether or not they count.

Traffic Court Issues

No one wants to get into a traffic court, but it is something that could happen to anyone. However, those instances are not going to appear on your credit report because those traffic-related issues focus on your driving issues and not your finances.

The impact on your finances could still impact your credit rating if you use your credit card to cover the expenses associated with paying the fines for traffic violations.

The only court-related considerations that you might find on your credit report are expenses relating to the financial obligations you have. These include judgments where you might have been ordered to pay.

Support Obligations

You might have many obligations relating to your family or children. These include things relating to your family's health, education expenses, and so forth. Most forms of family or child support are not going to appear on your credit history report.

All of these points show that not everything in your life is going to be reported on your credit report. The odds are some expenses will not make an impact on your credit data.

Chapter 6 – What Makes the Three Credit Reporting Bureaus Different?

People in the United States will have their credit data collected by three companies – Equifax, Experian, and TransUnion. These groups all have the same objective of capturing and reporting the credit histories and information of people.

The important thing to notice about these bureaus is that they all have specific terms for how they will look at your credit history. If you compare your score between all three groups, you might notice that they are all different.

This chapter focuses on looking at why your credit history can be different on all three of these companies. Each company is regulated by the Fair Credit Reporting Act.

The Three Groups

Let's take a look at these three groups to understand how they report. These are groups that are trusted in the field of finance.

Experian

Experian was formed in 1996 in Dublin.

When you look at your Experian report, you will notice something called your Status Details. This refers to details on when a negative item on your credit report will disappear. Experian lets you know when those negative things are going to be removed, thus allowing you to plan to resolve credit problems.

The Balance History section of an Experian report includes details on the balances of your credit lines. This includes details on the balance you held on a line and the maximum balance you could have held. The details provide you with simple information on what you are doing with your finances at any given time.

Experian has also grown over time to become a popular group that also offers credit monitoring services. These include solutions to help people manage their identity information and to help them to recover from identity theft.

It is true that Experian is an Irish company, but it does not favor one country over another. Most of the people who use the services of Experian are from the United States.

Equifax

Equifax is a group that has focused on credit risk reviews for generations. Formed in 1899, the Atlanta-based group concentrates on identifying what people are doing with their credit. The organization has expanded in popularity and today it is listed on the New York Stock Exchange with the EFX symbol.

Equifax focuses on producing simple and easy to review profiles. You can review the Open and Closed Accounts sections on your Equifax report to see what is active and what you might need to repair. All the information is listed in alphabetical order.

Your credit accounts are also organized with an 81-month history. You can use this extensive history to see all the payments you have made on your accounts, what you owed, and what you owe now. Sometimes an 81-month history might not be available due to your account not having enough data available to produce a report of that length.

TransUnion

TransUnion was formed in 1968, but it is still valuable and important. It is so important that TransUnion has an NYSE listing as TRU.

Although TransUnion is considered to be the smallest of the three bureaus, the size of TransUnion is still valuable. The group has revenues of about $1 billion each year.

TransUnion's reports are more thorough than the others. It has information on everything relating to your employment including details on the specific position you hold with a business when you were hired, and so forth. Details on when you opened certain lines of credit can also be found and the specific types of lines of credit.

One thing you might notice on a TransUnion report is a series of colored boxes. These state that your account is either Satisfactory or Unsatisfactory. This refers to whether you have been on-time with your payments and that you are properly managing your finances.

You will notice six types of boxes on a TransUnion report surrounding one of your credit lines. These boxes make it easier for you to review your report:

1. A green box states that your account is current and that you are making regular payments.

2. A yellow box states that you are 30 days late on a payment.

3. An orange box shows that you are 60 days late on that payment.

4. A red box may have 90 on it. This means you have been 90 days or more late on a payment.

5. A red box with a 120 means you are at least 120 days late on a payment.

6. A white box with an X states that details on your account are unknown.

The system is convenient as it gives you all the details you need to know about what you are getting yourself into when managing your payments and seeing what has to be covered the soonest.

Why Would Your Score Be Different With Each Bureau?

You might notice that your scores on these three credit reports are different from one another. For instance, you might see that your Experian account has a rating of 680. Meanwhile, your TransUnion score is 690 while your Equifax account has a 675 total.

The fact is that each of these groups has their own value system. Each of these three reporting entities has specific standards for how they value different points on your account. Those standards are kept confidential, so you would have to focus on an all-around approach to repairing and maintaining your credit.

However, you can always identify an error in your report if you ever notice that you have a dramatic shift in the value of your score between certain reports. For instance, you might notice that you have a score of 700 on your TransUnion report versus a score of 630 on your Experian report. This could be a sign that something is wrong with your Experian account and that you need to get the issue resolved soon.

You would have to review each of those credit reports accordingly to determine what the issue is. Sometimes there might be a case where one bureau is late on giving you an update.

Which Reports Will Employers, Creditors, and Others Review?

One point about your three reports is that different groups will analyze specific reports from these various groups. Although all three of these reports are equally critical to your credit history, you should still review the reports to see what is reported on them.

The individual creditors and employers will typically review all three of these reports. They will do this to get a fair idea of what your financial status is.

You should review each carefully. Remember that the reports that each of these three groups offers are different from one another, but they are all valuable.

Chapter 7 – The Range of Credit Scores

A higher credit score is always positive. Those who have higher scores are easier to trust when it comes to money.

A score will go from 300 to 850. This is in accordance with FICO standards. Each group that reviews your credit will use different score ranges to determine your ability to handle credit.

The Five Levels

Your FICO score will be divided based on one of five ranges from 300 to 850. These ranges are used to determine how well a person can handle certain credit-related functions.

1. Very Poor – 300-579

The lowest level is the Very Poor level. Those who have credit ratings under 580 will often have to pay high interest rates or fees for certain financial services. This is provided that those people are approved for credit, to begin with. At this juncture, you are more likely to be rejected for credit.

2. Fair – 580-669

Most people in the United States have a Fair credit rating. A little more than 20 percent of people will have this rating level. At this point, a person is seen as a subprime borrower. That person can apply for a loan or other item and get it, but the rating might prove to be too hard to manage.

3. Good – 670-739

Around 20 percent of the people in the country have a Good rating. A person with a Good rating will not be considered likely to become delinquent. The fees and rates for someone with a Good rating might still be high.

4. Very Good – 740-799

A Very Good rating will likely be considered for a better rate and will most likely be approved for credit.

5. Strong – 800-850

Those who have the best possible credit will likely get the prime rates for their financial dealings. A person with this credit rating will be considered a minimal risk.

What Score Do You Need?

In most cases, you might need to have a credit score of 500 to get access to certain financial services. That is, the odds of someone being refused will be dramatically reduced after that person reaches the 500 mark.

You might need a higher score if you want to arrange to finance an auto or mortgage loan. The Federal Housing Administration would require you to have a larger score of at least 580 to be approved for a mortgage loan with a 3.5% down payment. Those who have a credit score under 580 could still apply for a loan, but a 10% down payment would be required.

What Hurts Your Credit Score?

There is another thing to note surrounding one's credit score and how it is influenced. The threat involved with certain problems can be dramatic.

Here are a few of the things to consider with regards to negative issues that might affect someone's credit report.

- Missed credit card payment: 60-90 point drop

- Missed auto loan payment: 60-100 point drop

- Missed mortgage loan payment: 60-100 point drop

- Maxing out a credit card: 50-100 point drop

- Bankruptcy – at least 150 fewer points on your credit rating

The actual results of such things will vary based on one's credit history, the intensity of the situation, and how often certain problems have occurred. A person with a small missed payment who has not had many misses in the past could have a minimal drop in score. Those who regularly struggle to keep their payments current should expect their scores to decline quite quickly.

What Change Can Your Credit Score Cause?

The change in your credit score can mean the difference between a prime rate and a nonprime rate of interest.

Let's suppose you're going to apply for a car loan of $30,000 amortized over 60 months. If you had a score of about 650, you might get a loan rate of 6.5%. You would pay $5,219 in interest over the course of your loan. That would amount to an estimated monthly payment of $587 on average.

Now let's say you had a credit rating of 750 and you were going for the same car loan. You could get a prime rate of 3.5% on your loan. This would result in $2,745 in interest payments on your loan with a monthly payment of $546.

Getting a better credit rating can help you in lessening the interest rates for your loan.

How Long Does It Take to Get a Better Credit Rating?

The amount of time it takes to get to the Strong credit rating range varies. It could take several years for someone to reach this level. A person would have to do the following to get the best credit rating possible:

1. Keep making payments on-time. These include payments on one's loans and credit cards.

2. Make sure the debts are under control. This includes making sure one does not charge more to one's credit accounts than necessary.

3. Keep the same credit lines open for as long as possible. Loyalty is not going to be worth as much as making payments on-time, but loyalty can still make a difference.

What Credit Rating Will You Start With?

Those who do not have a credit history will spend more money on their expenses because they have not proven themselves to be financially responsible yet. What is a person's credit rating going to be when starting out?

The truth is that a person who has no credit will not actually have a credit score. That is, the person is not going to have a credit rating of 300 at the start. Rather, a person will work toward managing a better score over time.

After a few months of making regular payments on debts, you might notice that your credit rating will start to improve. You might have a rating of 500 at the start, but at the same time that might move up to 600.

Chapter 8 – The Various Credit Scores

FICO uses many scores that relate to specific types of credit-related functions and you must look at the scores when you are applying for certain types of investments.

The scores in question focus mainly on how well you are able to cover certain debts. There are no guarantees that every credit score is going to be reviewed by a creditor.

Auto Lending Score

An auto lending score is based on how well you are able to pay off auto-related expenses including charges relating to an auto loan or insurance. The key is to have payments for auto-related costs on-time without adding more interest than necessary.

The score may impact your ability to be approved for a car loan. You might find that a group will be very inquisitive over how well you are able to pay off your loan. When you show that you have a strong history of paying auto-related debts, you will find you could get a higher value car loan.

Credit Card Application Score

A credit card score focuses on how well a person can cover the expenses associated with a credit card. Part of this includes seeing how well a person can pay off a card without incurring extra fees or interest charges.

Credit card companies and banks are especially interested in this score because they know that many of the services they offer entail unsecured debts. It could be very easy for a card company to lose money when it notices that you aren't paying off your debts on-time. Companies are not going to want to deal with people who are deemed risky.

Mortgage Lending Score

A mortgage lending score focuses on how well a person can pay off a mortgage loan or other investment. A home will cost hundreds of thousands of dollars in most cases. A group will want to ensure that a borrower can pay off the expenses in question within the amortized length of the loan.

Your mortgage lending score may also help you get a new rate on a mortgage loan. The lower interest rate on a loan could be critical to reduce your borrowing rate or to keep monthly payments from becoming exorbitant.

Chapter 9 – Marriage and Your Credit Report

You might think that by getting married, you would make it easier for you to have a better credit report. The truth is that getting married will not necessarily improve your credit. Even if you had a joint account with your partner, you are still going to have separate credit scores.

This chapter focuses mainly on marriage and how it can influence one's credit rating, but it can also be applicable to anyone who wants to get a joint account or other shared account. Marriage is often the most common reason why joint accounts are formed.

Will Your Credit Reports Merge Upon Marriage?

It is not true your credit report will merge with your new spouse's report after you are married. This is probably the most popular myth people have when it comes to credit and marriage.

Although two people are officially in a union upon marriage, they are still specific individuals. They are not going to be judged on their financial actions based on what they do together.

All credit reports are based on Social Security Numbers. These SSNs are not going to merge when two people marry. Instead, those numbers are kept separate along with the credit reports that are attached to them. In other words, a person who has bad credit is not going to suddenly have good credit after that someone gets married.

Is Marriage Going to Harm Someone's Credit Score?

People are often worried that a marriage might harm their credit ratings because of the expenses that might occur as a result of the marriage. These expenses often include costs relating to the wedding, honeymoon, reception, moving in, and other things.

While there are various expenses associated with a wedding, those costs are not necessarily going to cause a person to lose points on one's credit rating provided they are paid off on-time. The expenses associated with marriage will be treated exactly same as any other debt. Therefore, it is best for a person to be astute and prompt when paying for those expenses.

Will Your Credit History Be Changed if your Legal Name Is Changed?

Women often have their last names legally changed when they are married. This is not going to affect her credit history. A negative history under her old name will not be erased, nor will she have to worry about a good history disappearing.

When a woman changes her name following a marriage, her maiden name will still be on her existing credit report. Her new married name will be used as an alias.

A newly married woman should be aware of any errors or other inaccuracies that might appear on her credit report after her marriage becomes official. It might some time for the report to reflect her new name.

Will a Spouse Automatically Become a Joint User on Someone's Accounts?

Many people are worried about their individual accounts becoming joint accounts following a marriage. This would not happen unless a spouse asks to be on someone's account.

You can be added to your spouse's credit cards or other accounts by using the appropriate application. Ask your creditor to be added to your spouse's account to make it into a joint account if you wish. The application process to make an account a joint account will vary based on the company.

Chapter 10 – Joint Account Considerations

A joint account entails two or more people being linked to the same line of credit. In most cases, a joint account would involve two people who may or may not be married using the same card. This is provided that the two people agree to have a joint account.

Multiple business partners may also have an account like this. Those partners will contact each other with the intention of making it easier for them to manage their funds and make them work as needed.

You could use a joint account to get your credit to grow. This can occur when you are working with another person who may assist you to build your credit.

The simplicity involved with a credit account can become hard to manage when you are not responsible with it.

Three Types of Accounts

The term "joint account" is technically a catch-all term for all the types of accounts you could use to obtain credit. There are three types of joint accounts:

1. Joint Credit

A joint credit refers to when you are a partner on a credit line. You have as much control over that line as another person. This is the most common type of joint account as it works well for married couples, business partners, and others who have close relationships with one another.

With a joint credit line, you and another person have signed to a credit application for a single card or loan. The account will have your name on it as well as the name of the other person who signed for it with you. The people named on that credit line can use the funds on it as they wish.

This does not mean that the bill can be split in any way. Everyone on the account is fully responsible for making payments. You are responsible for paying what someone else spends on that account. That other person is responsible for what you spend too.

2. Authorized User

An authorized user account is listed to use the credit involved, but they do not have any responsibility with paying it off. That person did not sign an application for access. You are simply being given permission by the main holder of the account to use that line of credit.

These include people that you are regularly close to that you might be willing to entrust in using your credit line.

Whoever holds the account will be responsible for repayment. The holder would have to contact the users about getting paid privately.

When the account holder does not make payments, the creditor may contact the authorized users about the charges. This can legally happen to cover the debts on the account.

3. Co-Signer

A co-signer stipulates to be responsible for repayment if the account holder does not make the payments. The most common example of co-signing is when a parent co-signs for an account that is held by a child. A teenager might have a new credit card, but the parent would co-sign for the account. The teen would have to pay off the bills on that credit card. If that teen does not pay what is owed, the co-signer is responsible for the payments. This can be risky

Why Consider a Joint Credit Account?

Having a joint account can work well for many reasons:

1. It is easier for people on a joint account to track their cash flow.

A joint account allows people to review the debts that they have and when they are being paid off as needed. This works well for married couples and other groups that want to ensure they will get their accounts managed correctly.

2. The bank fees could be reduced based on the certain accounts being opened.

Individual bank accounts can come with fees. However, with a joint account, it becomes easier for multiple people to handle those fees. They can divide the fees between each other evenly. The fees associated may vary by group.

3. People with joint accounts will also have better relationships with one another.

A marriage or other partnership is designed to be about trust. A joint account allows people to trust each other about what they are doing with their credit.

4. Everyone will be accountable when handling an account.

Accountability is vital for handling expenses. A joint account ensures that all people involved are accountable and will pay off their charges as needed.

The Risks of a Joint Account

Having a joint account can be worthwhile when all is considered, but there are several risks associated with a joint account:

1. There is a chance that someone might incur an overdraft.

With so many people associated with a joint account, there is a chance that someone might incur an overdraft. This occurs when a person goes above the limit on the account. This will cause overdraft fees and possibly extra interest charged on the account.

Having too many incidents of overdrafts will cause your credit score to be harmed. This might happen even when you are not responsible for whatever is happening on your account.

2. Your money in your account might be targeted by creditors if a joint holder becomes involved in legal trouble.

3. You may inherit someone's debts when you have a joint account.

When you enter into a joint account, you will be involved with the other person's financial affairs. This includes the debts they have before you joined accounts.

4. A divorce, separation, or death could be difficult.

Many bills and other expenses associated with a joint account might be difficult to pay off when someone leaves the union and are no longer a joint holder of the account. These include costs relating to divorce, separation, or death.

Before Making a Joint Account

People must look at how their accounts are organized if they want to have easier times with managing their credit profiles. You could benefit from being a part of a joint account, but even then you must be cautious.

Several things must be considered before you enter into a joint account:

1. Look at the value of the credit.

The credit in the joint account might have a certain limit. Be aware of what that limit is so you can ensure no one is going to spend beyond that total.

2. Establish a line of communication between yourself and other people who have access to the account.

This includes deciding who is going to spend money on that joint account and what will be included.

3. Prepare ground rules for how the credit line is to be used.

Everyone associated with the credit line should be consulted about how that line will be used and who will be using it and for what. Certain limits for what people are going to spend should be established.

4. Look at how responsible the people associated with an account are.

The people involved with the account should be responsible and careful with whatever it is they are using.

Do not have a joint account with someone who might not understand how it works. Talking with someone about an account based on one's effort in handling it and spending right is critical. Of course, it always helps to work with people who have experience handling credit. People with great credit scores can help you with a joint account, but those whose credit is not good could be a hindrance and a risk.

5. Understand how the credit line can be paid off.

You might enter into a credit line where you can pay it off online. The people with whom you make arrangements for the joint account should be consulted as well as how the line may be paid. It might also help to talk about the types of payments that can be made and how they may be scheduled.

6. Review the value of the credit line.

A high-value joint account can be risky when you consider the money associated with it and the people involved with using it. You might be better off having a smaller joint account at the start so you can get used to the concept while ensuring the risks of irresponsible partners would be minimal. Later, you can consider applying for a larger credit limit.

What Can the Courts Do With Your Account?

There are often times when a court might demand that someone pays a certain amount of money to keep an account running. A court might request a person covers a certain amount of money based on the amount owed on the account. The people in a joint account who are concerned can have a court order issued to require one of the joint owners of the account to make payment on the account. A court does not have the right to move debts from one partner to another in the event of a divorce or dissolution of the account. All persons in the joint account would still be responsible for paying off whatever is owed on that debt.

The Most Important Part of Having a Joint Account

The most important rule associated with a joint account is you will ultimately be responsible for everything that you charge on that account.

You will be partially responsible for what other people spend on the account as well. You will have to watch how you're handling your payments on a joint account by looking at what you are spending and pooling the appropriate amount.

A joint account can help you to have a better credit rating if you continue to look after your debts appropriately and on-time.

Chapter 11 – How to Obtain and Read Your Credit Report

Getting a copy of your credit report is the first thing to do when looking for information on how to repair your credit.

You are legally entitled to have a free credit report once a year from each of the three reporting bureaus. The organizations will provide you with this support to ensure that you have the information you need.

Obtaining the Report

The first thing to do is to get your credit report. You need to get all three of your reports so you can ensure you have a clear idea of what your credit rating is like. Remember that each credit reporting group operates differently and that there's a chance one report might be different from another.

The process for getting your credit report is:

1. You can visit annualcreditreport.com to get your report.

This is the only website that you can get your legitimate credit reports. The site has partnered with all three reporting groups to ensure you can get the reporting data that you want.

Avoid any other site that claims they will provide you with free credit reports. These places are often either scams or are in the hopes of taking more of your money off you. These include places that claim to offer regular monitoring services that could cost more to use than what those services are generally worth.

2. You can also call 1-877-322-8228 for help.

This phone number links to the Federal Trade Commission that will provide help to you to obtain your reports. You can use this number at any time of the day to get your reports sent to you by mail.

You must also provide the following information to confirm your identity:

- Your name

- Your address

- Your Social Security Number

- Your date of birth

These details will confirm that you are the one asking for your credit report.

Reading Your Report

There are four sections on your credit report to review:

1. Identifying Details

The first section is your identity. Every detail of the report must be accurate. An important part of this section involves the extensive variety of details including some details that you might not have expected to find on a credit report, such as:

- Details you listed when applying for the report

- Telephone numbers linked to your name; these include home and mobile numbers

- Details about your employer

- Your spouse's name and the names of any other person who might be directly related to you

Why is all this information listed on your report? Different people will have reported about you in various ways. Different credit reporting groups will have information about you received by various means. In fact, some groups might have spelled your name differently, and this needs to be corrected.

You always have the option to file a dispute over how your name is listed if you wish. Details on how to file a dispute with someone will be listed later in this guide.

2. Your Credit History

Details on how your credit is laid out should be checked accordingly. Your credit accounts may be referred to as trade lines. Each individual account you have from a single creditor may be listed at this point.

Your report will include the following details:

- The type of credit that you have

- The group that your credit is listed with

- The identity of whoever is holding the account; this may include both you and other people related to you

- The amount of money owing on your account

- How often your payments are made; this includes details on when you have to make payments

- Minimum payment amounts

- The status of your account; it may be open or closed, paid or unpaid

- How you are making payments and if they are on-time or late

- The amount of money you are spending on specific items each month; this point is relevant for Experian and TransUnion accounts

- Information on internal collections, closures of account, and anything else relating to your accounts

You must check on each part of your report to see that the details of that report are accurate.

Also, this section will be as long as it includes several years of data relating to your credit.

3. Public Records

The public records refer to anything listed in your name regarding the struggles you had toward paying off your debts.

Public records are essentially red flags that relate to your inability to handle your credit. These include:

- Bankruptcies

- Tax Liens

- Foreclosures

- Judgments

Details on lawsuits or arrests in your name will not be listed.

The most important part of these public records is that they will remain on your record for years to come. Getting your credit repaired often entails having these problems removed from your account, but there are no guarantees that you will be able to get these removed.

4. Inquiries

The last section is the inquiries that have been made on your credit report. You will see both hard and soft inquiries.

A hard inquiry is an inquiry that you initiated. This is when you asked to get a review of your credit report.

A soft inquiry occurs when someone pre-screens you for any reason. This includes cases where a company pre-screens you to see if you are suitable for handling certain financial functions. Possible employers may also use soft inquiries to get a clear idea of your financial status.

With the inquiry readout, you will get information on everything relating to how well your credit report is analyzed.

These credit reports will be provided to you for free once a year. Also, checking your credit report is not going to impact your score.

What If You Need Another Report?

You have the right to get one free credit report from each of these bureaus.

You have the right to get multiple reports from these groups throughout the year, but there will be a cost. Specifically, you might have to pay around $10 to $20 for each credit report you get during the year after the free copy.

You can get one of these reports by sending your data to Experian, Equifax, and TransUnion. Each group has its own website and address. You must talk directly with these groups to get the credit report that you want.

There is a cost if you joined some program that promises various debt management and credit monitoring functions.

The problem with many of these groups that claim to offer special credit monitoring is that they will often charge you more than what you might spend if you put in an effort on your own.

Why Get Multiple Reports?

Getting more than one of these reports is a good idea for you as it ensures that you can judge how accurate your reports are based on any substantial changes that you might have produced on your credit profile. You can ask for them every two to three months if needed. This should be enough time to repair your credit and pay off your debts.

More importantly, these reports will help you to identify cases of identity fraud. Even as you work on managing your credit, your identity could still be at risk of being exposed in some form. A person could use your Social Security Number and use it to open a financial investment or service.

You should at least keep those reviews spaced out well enough so you can identify the changes that appear on your report.

Getting A Free Report Following a Rejection

Although the cost of getting an additional credit report isn't much when the big picture is considered, you should be aware of when you could qualify to get a free report. You may get a free report in the event that someone has taken an action against you with regards to your credit. You can get a free report in the event of any of these situations:

- You are turned down for a new line of credit.

- An insurance company refuses to give you coverage.

- You are denied acceptance of a new job.

Ask for a report within 60 days of that notice occurring. You must consult each of the individual credit reporting companies with details surrounding the rejection or another credit-related issue so the report would be free. The companies will provide help to see why you are being declined coverage or service.

Other Cases When You Can Get a Free Report

There are many other instances that will allow you to obtain a free credit report within a year's time. These are times that have nothing to do with being rejected:

- You are unemployed and you plan to look for a new job within the next 60 days. Provide details of your job search or what might have caused you to become unemployed.

- You are on welfare; you must have proof of your welfare status.

- You have been impacted by identity theft. Details on any fraud or other negative situations should be relayed to the bureau.

Again, you would have to contact the three individual credit reporting companies to get your reports separately.

Should You Get All Three Bureaus at Once?

It may be a good idea for you to get your credit report from each of the three bureaus at the same time. It is understandable that you would normally want to get these three reports spread out over the course of a year. These bureaus report things so differently from one another that it is best for you to get your reports at the same time just to be safe. After all, you never know when one of the three might feature a significant error that you can resolve.

As mentioned earlier, the ways how these three credit bureaus will report your score and manage it will vary based on many points that are kept secret. There is always a chance that certain things will change and make it harder for you to manage your credit.

Simply ordering these at the same time each year is always smart to make it easier for you to afford.

Now that you understand the value of your credit report and how to get and read it, you can work toward resolving the issues that you might find on your reports. The next chapter concentrates on what you can do to resolve the disputes and other concerns that you might come across as you look through your report.

Chapter 12 – Using the Fair Credit Reporting Act

One of the best parts of managing your credit repair plans is knowing that you're not alone when it comes to your credit. There are many laws that have been passed by the American government that will help you. These laws are designed to help you get your credit organized. The best part of these rules is that they are all simple and easy to follow.

The first of these laws to look at is the Fair Credit Reporting Act. The Act states that all the information that is to be collected regarding your credit will be handled fairly and without any bias or other problems.

The FCRA has been in force since 1970. It was designed as an amendment to the Federal Deposit Insurance Act. This was designed to require banks and other insured organizations to maintain proper records and to ensure there are no problems with having certain debts managed.

The specific thing about the FCRA that makes it special is that the Act focuses on regulating consumer reporting groups, particularly TransUnion, Experian, and Equifax. People who use those groups to get credit reports will also be protected by the Act.

The general goal of the Act is to ensure that customers' credit reports are fair and that reporting organizations are not biased against one group. The intention is to keep all reports fair and neutral without judgments against anyone who might owe money.

A consumer has the right to have one's credit report accurately and fairly used. While it is true that a credit report might have negative information, the report must still be accurate.

You might find cases where there is an error on your report. You can use the FCRA to ask for a review of those errors on your report. Details on how to dispute something on your credit report will be discussed in the next chapter.

Access to a Credit Report

A credit bureau will have a series of restrictions and requirements that must be followed. A person does have the right to access a credit report of any person for credit or background checks. To have access to a credit report, the following applies:

- A person can only acquire a credit report in accordance with the purposes that the FCRA has regulated access to them.

For instance, a person can use a credit report for a background check on someone who wants to use some financial investment. A business may also use this to discover how well a person can pay off debts before offering financial services or allowing a person to make a sizable purchase. The reason for the request has to be logical while also being fair on the person being investigated.

- A person or entity must let the customer know when some kind of action is taken based on something found on a report.

For instance, a business would have to let a person know when they are being rejected because of something found on a credit report.

- The names of companies or other entities that asked for the credit report must be provided to the consumer.

The consumer must be given the information regarding who has requested the credit report. It is even more important to know why you have been rejected because of something on your report.

How a Background Check Works

The FCRA states that you could be subjected to a background check based on your credit report, but you give permission to have a credit check performed on your name.

The FCRA states that you can allow someone to perform a background check to discover what is happening with your financial data.

There are a few things that have to be done when it comes to allowing a background check:

- An entity must get your permission to perform a background check.

Express written permission must be provided. Always review the fine print.

- The entity must tell you how your credit report will be used.

Whether it entails reviewing your financial history or your current ability to manage debts, they must explain to you why a credit report is required. This is to give you the confidence in knowing that your data will be used responsibly.

- The information in the report must not be misused.

The purposes for using the information should be precisely what that group is going to do with it and that it will not be shared with any other company.

- A copy of your report is to be provided in the event that you are not supported in some way.

If you are rejected for some financial service or job, you should be given the right to get your credit report for free.

- You should also have the opportunity to dispute the information on the report in the event that you have some concern about the report.

You have to be given a copy of your credit report before you can dispute how it was used to reject your application for credit or a job.

The terms associated with handling an inquiry are regulated by the FCRA as a means of creating a sense of fairness and control over how one's data is to be used.

Why Get a Free Report?

Your ability to get a free report from each of the three reporting bureaus every year is regulated by the FCRA.

The FCRA offers this free report service to ensure that all of the credit bureaus are honest about the content of your report and so that you can get resolve errors.

These bureaus can make honest mistakes. After all, they are working with lots of information on millions of people. You need to make sure such errors are found and can be managed and corrected. The FCRA provides people with the ability to get those errors resolved without problems developing.

Removing Negative Items

There is a chance that you might come across some negative items on your report. You can use the FCRA to help you get those items removed. The process to do this is:

1. When you send out a request to a bureau about an error, that bureau will be obligated to review that error.

The FCRA places the law on your side as you have right to have any problems surrounding your account reviewed and corrected.

2. The bureau in question will have to remove the questionable item on your report if the bureau finds that it is inaccurate.

3. There is a chance that the bureau might find that the item removed might actually be correct. If that happens, the bureau does not necessarily have to add that negative item back into your report. However, the bureau would have to tell you with at least five days' notice if this has to be done.

There is often a chance for a bureau to put a negative item back onto your account if it is deemed too valuable or might be critical in nature. You should at least be given the opportunity to know what is to be added back onto your account before this happens.

The timeframe for when something is removed and when it is added should be short.

4. The FCRA states that any negative items that are found on your report can only last for a certain period of time.

The FCRA states that any negative things on your report are removed after seven years.

Bankruptcy is the exception to this part of the FCRA. A bankruptcy will stay on your report for ten years.

Correcting Errors

There are three points about correcting errors in accordance with the FCRA:

1. The group should correct any problems that you identify on your report within 30 days after the error was reported.

2. There might be cases where a bureau states that an error is accurate. The bureau must give an explanation of this within 30 days.

3. A group that will report a negative item to someone will have to give you 30 days' notice.

What If Your Rights Are Violated?

If you may experience a violation of your rights, you can recover damages in the event that someone breaks the rules of the FCRA. This can include instances of someone asking for a background check on your credit without your permission or someone refuses to let you dispute an error.

You can recover damages that could help you pay off debts but also to have something on your credit report removed if you can prove that someone broke FCRA rules.

You would have to go through a court hearing. You should not have to pay any substantial legal fees because the FCRA will allow for those to be covered as needed.

There are a few steps to protect your rights with the FCRA:

1. Review the error on your report. Make sure the content is accurate and detailed.

2. Check if someone from one of the bureaus has refused to look at the report in question.

3. Contact a lawyer to help get the FCRA to work for you. In this case, you might have to talk with a lawyer about suing the credit bureau over the situation. In this case, a consumer rights attorney may be contacted.

4. Initiate the case within the statute of limitations.

Be sure that you contact the legal team to resolve the problem resolved within two years after the violation has been found or five years after the violation took place.

5. Prepare information in the court case about the content being disputed or discussed within the case. This includes all the data relating to your financial situation and how it is to be discussed in a court of law.

6. The case should review what is happening within your account and what can be done to manage certain problems on your account.

After the case is reviewed, the bureau should provide you with:

- The error in question should be properly corrected. This includes having the error removed from your report, thus improving your score.

- You can recover damages caused by the error. This includes damages over any losses that happened because your credit score is wrong.

The amount of the judgment will vary based on the situation. You are legally entitled to collect at least $2,500, although you might be able to recover more.

- Any punitive damages may be recovered.

- Legal fees and other costs in the case will be covered.

You can have the issue disputed in a court if the group does not respond to your request to review an error or if some other FCRA-related violation occurred. The time involved could be lengthy.

Be aware though that the legal situation must only be considered if the traditional process for removing an error does not work. You need to use the general dispute process that will be covered in the next chapter first.

Chapter 13 – Handling a Dispute About Your Credit Report

The information on your credit report is critical, but there is always the chance that your credit report might have some kind of error. It only takes one error on your report to cause havoc to your credit score.

There is always a chance for one of the credit bureaus will record something that is inaccurate. These unintentional mistakes can cost someone a sizable amount of money and credit points if they occur.

You must get any of these errors that might show up on your credit report resolved as soon as possible.

The process of managing disputes on your credit report is covered in accordance with the Fair Credit Reporting Act. The Act gives you the right to dispute anything on your report.

Common Errors

The kinds of errors you might come across when reviewing your credit report can be varied. There is a strong chance that you might come across a legitimate issue on your report.

In a 2012 study, the Federal Trade Commission found that nearly a quarter of all Americans have at least one error on one of their credit reports. This statistic shows that the credit reporting groups clearly have lots of work to do when determining what people have on their reports, but at the same time those groups are not always going to be fully equipped to resolve those issues.

Some of the common errors you might find on your report include the following:

- You might have a credit application that was from someone with a name similar to yours. This application could be erroneously included on your credit report.

- A clerical error might have happened due to a hand-written application. It is often easy for people to make mistakes when calculating hand-written data.

- An inaccurate identifying number was used on an account. This could include the incorrect credit card number, bank account number, or Social Security Number.

- A card or loan payment was not listed. This could have included a payment going onto the wrong person's account.

Whatever the case may be, such problems can be significant and could hurt your credit rating. You must look carefully at every part of your credit reports to see that there are no issues.

Steps to Resolve an Error

To resolve an error, these steps should be used for each of the credit reports you have:

1. Identify the error on your report.

Check every single detail on the report to ensure there are no errors. When you do find even the smallest problem, you can proceed with this process.

2. Review the other reports to see if the problem is consistent.

The reports should be checked to make sure they are as identical as possible. You have to only manage an error in the case where the issue is the same in all of the reports you.

3. Send a letter to the credit bureau that has reported the information that is incorrect.

You can send a letter online or by mail to any of the three groups. Refer to later in the chapter for details on preparing the letter.

4. Contact the group or individual that provided the erroneous information to the reporting bureau.

You can talk with the creditor that initiated the error to get confirmation about the issue or to discuss the problem. This step may help in the event that you have some problem with your report that has nothing to do with your identity but might be due to some error in the process of entering details on your report.

This step is not necessary for every situation. Any identity-related problems on your report can be discussed directly with the bureau instead of with your creditor.

5. Prepare the proper attachments associated with the issue.

Include physical copies of any payments or other things you have done with your credit. This is if you're sending a physical letter.

For cases where you will send everything online, include supporting documents as attachments.

6. Wait for 45 days for the credit reporting bureau to respond to you.

You need to give the bureau time to review your error. The credit bureau should have about 30 days to review your dispute. After the review, the bureau will have about five days to get its results back to you. This is to give the bureau the opportunity to produce a proper response.

The response should include one of three results. These will be discussed next.

The Three Possible Results of a Dispute

The bureau must have time to contact the person or company that reported something to be placed on your file or time to analyze the contents you have sent. The bureau should then give you a sensible response. The reply has to be as detailed and thorough as possible. There are three possible responses from the bureau:

1. Correct

A correct response occurs when the bureau finds that you are accurate and that the bureau made a mistake on your report. The bureau should give you the results of the research and also a new copy of your credit report with the correction intact.

The bureau should also provide you with information on the furnishing party that had the wrong information. This will help you identify who you might need to avoid in the future.

2. Incorrect

The bureau may find that your argument was incorrect and that there is no need for your credit report to be changed. You should be given information on the situation and how the bureau determined that your account was not inaccurate.

3. Frivolous

A frivolous dispute takes place when you have sent incorrect or incomplete information. This may also include cases where you have tried to dispute an issue many times. Although you have the option to submit the dispute once again with new materials at this point, there is a chance the bureau may not respond to the request to review the case again.

The letter you receive from the bureau should give you all the details you need to know about the dispute and the problems you might have with it.

Preparing a Letter

The letter has to be thorough, detailed, and offer proof that an error has been made on your credit report.

Include the following:

1. All your identifying information.

    -   Your full name

    -   Your address

    -   The ID number on your report

    -   Your date of birth

    -   Your driver's license number

    -   Your Social Security Number

    -   The date that you are writing the letter

2. Add details of the credit bureau involved with the error.

List the specific name of the company and the address. You can add details about the company's website if you wish.

3. Introduce the letter by stating that you are disputing something listed on your account.

4. List the specific details about the item you are disputing.

- The account number of the error you are disputing

- The dates surrounding the information you are disputing

- Details on the inaccuracy

- Information on the company that provided the wrong information

- The type of information - a credit payment or inquiry etc.

5. Provide a list of enclosures under your signature.

6. Prepare the enclosures which provide proof of your claim of the error reported.

The above process will give the bureau all the details surrounding your dispute.

Be cordial and personal in your letter. You can include that you have been working with a credit line for a while but you also want to ensure that line is covered accordingly.

Don't be dramatic. Being overly emotional in your letter will make it harder for the bureau to accept your word or take the situation seriously.

Review Your Credit Report After the Dispute

You should not assume that your credit report will be corrected right away if you get a correct response from the bureau in question. Although you should get a copy of your report that shows the corrected issue, that does not mean that the problem will be corrected right away.

The update cycle at a credit bureau can take some time. It can take days or weeks for corrections to go through. Therefore, you should get a new copy of your credit report a few weeks or months after the issue had been resolved. Check on that new report to see if the problem was removed and if the credit score has been updated.

You can also get another version of your credit report a few months later if you prefer. You can use this to see that the change is final and that it has not been reversed or put back on your report.

You should contact the bureau in question and whoever gave the bureau inaccurate information in the event that you still notice the problem on your report.

What To Do If the Dispute Is Unsuccessful

There is always the chance that your dispute might not be resolved to your liking. There are a few things that you can do in the event that you get a negative response to your dispute.

1. Review the state of the error that you are disputing. The odds are the issue in question might not actually be an error.

One of the more common reasons why people have their disputes rejected is because they assume that the things they are disputing are things that can be analyzed. They think that these things do not have to be listed on a report, but the truth is that those details can, in fact, be listed.

2. Speak to the company that reported the incorrect information to the bureau.

Another reason for an unsuccessful dispute comes from someone choosing to only contact a bureau for help. Sometimes a person might not have contacted the credit card company or another group that reported the erroneous information in the first place. The credit bureau might assume that whatever the creditor reported is the truth.

3. Search for additional information on your dispute.

You might have to give the bureau more information about the dispute in question. This can include points relating to your credit history, any documents you have, or whatever else that might bolster your argument. You might come across new problems or concerns that could support your argument regarding your credit.

Filing a Complaint About the Dispute

You may still file a complaint regarding your dispute if you feel that you were not treated fairly or heard properly during the dispute process. You can send a complaint to the Consumer Financial Protection Bureau and can be found online at consumerfinance.gov.

You must make sure you have a sensible reason to argue even further. The reasons why a complaint may be filed can include the following:

- The process for reviewing your complaint took much longer than expected.

- The bureau did not treat you fairly during the review process. The bureau may have refused to answer your questions.

- The bureau might not have removed the inaccurate information properly. This could include if the error that was corrected did not show up on your report for four to six months after the problem was found.

You should not try to dispute the bureau's actions unless you are absolutely certain that there is a problem with the process of correcting the credit situation.

Chapter 14 – Using Section 609 to Your Advantage

When trying to clear errors off your credit report, it helps to have a sturdy loophole on hand to help you. One of the best loopholes you can use to repair your credit is Section 609.

A Section 609 letter can be filed if you feel that there is an issue surrounding your credit report that has to be reviewed and corrected.

Specifically, Section 609 can help you do more than just removing negative items on your credit report. It can also help you clear out closed accounts, charged off payments, and even details on public records. In other words, this section may be used to give you extra control over your credit reports.

Section 609 focuses on the verification of your content and what is being reported on your credit report. You can get any item removed from your report provided you use the right process for doing so.

This is a completely legal loophole that not everyone at the credit bureaus is aware of. Granted, some people at these bureaus might know about it, but they are taking advantage of the fact that hardly anyone uses it. By using Section 609 right, it becomes easier for all or at least a good portion of the negative items on an account to be resolved correctly and legally.

Section 609

Section 609 is a part of the Fair Credit Reporting Act that focuses on disclosures to consumers and how they may be used.

Section 609 states that a consumer reporting group must disclose various details to you when it comes to your credit. Section 609 requires the group to report on the following:

- Details on a consumer's credit file during a request

- The sources of information used to make a decision on credit ratings

- Identification of each entity that requested a consumer report for various purposes, particularly with employment intentions

- Details on any charges that one has to pay off or anything that someone might have failed to manage in one's account

- Inquiries that were received during that time period

- Cases where a consumer has requested information on one's credit score in the past

You have the right to see what it is on your report that makes it outstanding or what errors might need to be resolved.

Section 609 is that it is designed to help people understand what they are working with when it comes to their credit data and how it is to be handled.

There are often times when your report might not have the details that you wish it could have. At this point, you might need to contact someone who can help you resolve the problems for which you might not have received the proper notification.

Filing a Section 609 letter for cases where you were not given the proper notification surrounding your credit account can help you get the problem that listed on your report resolved as soon as possible.

This loophole for managing your credit is based on a simple concept. Let's say that you were in court for something that was charged against you. If the party suing you cannot prove their argument, you can get the dispute removed from your name.

A creditor is required by law to provide you with complete information on everything related to your account. You have to get this information from a creditor to help you resolve any problems that might come about on your account.

Verification and Electronic Documents

One valuable point about this loophole is how credit bureaus work with many electronic documents. That is, a creditor is not going to send information about negative things on your report by paper, but will instead explain all of these details electronically. Today, credit bureaus will not be able to review or verify signed documents or contracts before an item is reported on your credit report. There is a chance that a creditor could add something to a report without having any appropriate proof. Although the creditor is probably not going to be malicious and outright lie to a credit bureau, there is still the possibility that it could happen.

It helps to look at what a creditor will provide to a bureau. A creditor will send a monthly electronic file to a bureau that includes details on everything associated with an account. This includes details on the balance on a credit line, the payment term involved, the status of the account, any payment amounts that were sent, and so forth.

Each credit bureau will just assume that all the information regarding your account is accurate. The creditor is given the benefit of the doubt. Although many creditors might be honest, this is a point that could still be used to your benefit when it comes to your credit rating.

A credit bureau is paid to add items to credit reports. The worst part is that the bureau is not going to verify whatever is being added. This is the biggest problem with giving someone the benefit of the doubt and that does not always mean that what is being added to your report is correct.

This all leads to what may be the most important part of Section 609. Part e.2 states that there must be proper verification of the identity of a person and the claim being made. A bureau does not have to remove negative details from a report unless the content on the report cannot be verified.

Part b.2 also states that the details in the application for credit should be given to the customer. Information has to be verified in the application process to decide if a person can meet the criteria needed for managing certain credit-related functions.

There are often cases where creditors will take information on people without verified proof the information is accurate.

You can get a credit reporting bureau to show you the proof of verification of a negative item on your account. In this case, the item would have to be removed if the bureau does not have that verification on hand. Considering the tricks used by creditors and how bureaus receive money from those items, there is a possibility that you might have something negative on your report that cannot be verified. Therefore, you have the right to challenge that content on your report.

How to Write a Section 609 Letter

You will need to write a Section 609 letter to get your content reviewed by a bureau. Many bureaus do not get as many physical letters as they receive computer complaints. Many of those complaints are not actually read by the people at the firm. Instead, they are read by a computer that does not care about the truth.

The key to making your issue noticeable involves getting an actual person to read something. This includes using a certified letter that has to be opened and reviewed by someone. The letter will give the bureau all the details that need to be expressed while also being direct and specific.

You'll have to hand-write your content to make this work. This is because a bureau might take a printed letter and insert it into a scanning machine that will then identify the content. In other words, the group is not necessarily going to review the printed letter because the computer will do it for them.

That's why a hand-written letter is preferred. A machine is not able to read what is hand-written and it will still improve your chances of your letter being read.

The Information Needed for the Letter

The following information is needed to include in the letter:

1. Copies of the credit reports from the bureaus.

2. Review all the reports to see what negative items are included.

3. Create a list of all the negative items that were found. List information of the name of the account and the account number.

4. Find physical proof of verification surrounding the situation. For this letter, you need to show that there is no proof available for the negative items and they cannot be verified.

Writing the Letter to the Credit Bureaus

The process of writing a Section 609 letter will point out the errors on your credit report and how the problem can be resolved.

You will have to send your Section 609 letter to the credit bureau that you are trying to challenge. If all three bureaus are reporting the same error, you will have to send each of them the same letter but not at the same time.

1. Write the letter by hand in ink. Mail it to the billing department address of a bureau or all three bureaus. Use certified mail as this tracks your letter when it is received.

2. List the name on your account and the number that links to that account.

3. Explain to the creditor the item you are disputing. Include the particular code associated with the credit report.

   Discuss the reason you feel that the issue has to be removed. You may mention that the information has not been properly verified. Mention any documents or other attachments, including proof of payments you have made on the account in question.

For a Section 609 letter, the most important content is a copy of your credit report with the inaccurate information that cannot be verified highlighted. You can also let the bureau know what you want to have done about the error that you are disputing. In most cases, you might simply state a desire to have a problem on your report removed altogether or have the account adjusted to reflect the true status.

4. Provide copies of your driver's license and Social Security card.

5. After creating the letter, you can list the attachments (the old credit report or anything else proving that something cannot be verified as well as identification data) that you want to provide.

6. Address the envelope by hand. Do not type anything on the envelope.

The process here should work well for getting your content out to a bureau. More importantly, you are showing that you want to get certain problems resolved as soon as possible.

After a few weeks, you should receive a response from the bureau regarding what is happening with your account. In many cases, the negative items on your account can be removed altogether. Sometimes a few items might be removed but a couple others will still remain. You can see that your credit rating will improve if you follow the Section 609 process accordingly and thoroughly.

Writing a Section 609 Letter

You must be very cautious when writing a Section 609 letter. A few points to follow:

- Avoid disputing too many accounts on your report at one time.

You should avoid disputing more than twenty items on your account when working with your Section 609 letter. Any case where you dispute too many things could be interpreted as being frivolous. The bureau has the right to discard any dispute that it feels is frivolous.

- Certified mail is essential.

With a certified letter, you can track the delivery of the letter. Information stating that a credit bureau received your mail can be used in the event that the bureau does not review your initial request; a court may potentially remove the negative items from your report if it is found that the bureau ignored the request or just threw it out without acting upon it in accordance with FCRA standards.

- Avoid sending letters out to each of the credit bureaus at the same time.

After the letter is sent to the first bureau, wait about four to six business days to send the letter to the second bureau. Wait for another four to six business days to send the letter to the third bureau.

What If You Are Intimidated?

As useful as the Section 609 process can be, there is a chance that the bureau might try to intimidate you into dropping the challenge.

Specifically, a bureau may send a response stating that it received a request about your information that they considered suspicious. The bureau will say that it removed the request and that nothing was done with your account.

Sometimes the bureau can send you a questionnaire or other form surrounding the credit issue you have. This might be provided to you as a means of helping you to resolve the credit-related concerns you have. While this might sound like a nice gesture, this is a problem that could be a dramatic threat that could hurt you. You would have to send a new letter to the bureau reiterating what was in the first letter. This is to explain to the bureau that you are serious about the situation.

You must use the following steps:

1. Produce a new hand-written document for the message.

2. Explain that your concerns were refused on a certain date. State that you are serious about having certain problems reviewed.

3. Include the same details surrounding your credit profile.

4. Provide copies of the same identity-related documents that were sent out the first time.

5. Make sure the letter is certified. At this point, there is a realistic chance that a bureau might not want to hear from you once again and would surely discard that message you are trying to send out.

This process might require a concerted effort, but persistence is critical when it comes to getting the situation resolved.

In some cases, you might have to take in a third or fourth attempt to get the problem corrected. You have no real choice but to simply keep trying.

You might have no choice but to contact the Consumer Financial Protection Bureau for help. You would have to do this to discuss problems you have with the bureau that is not responding to you. Because you used certified mail, you can show that you definitely sent the letter and received negative responses from the bureau. The CFPB can represent you and eventually help you convince the credit bureaus that there is a legitimate problem associated with your accounts and credit report.

Be advised that this is not always going to work, but using the steps listed in this chapter will at least improve your chances to have your credit reports corrected.

Chapter 15 – Other Sections of the FCRA

There are many sections of the FCRA that can be utilized to help you fix your credit. These sections include many valuable loopholes that you can use to help you repair your credit rating. In other words, Section 609 was just the beginning.

Section 602

This part of the FCRA focuses on why the Act was produced. The Act was passed by the United States Congress as a means to protect people who might borrow funds or use any kind of financial service.

Section 608

Section 608 concentrates on the things that the government can review on your credit report. The government can review information of one's name, address, place of employment, and any former places of employment or addresses.

Section 610

Disclosure to consumers is listed in Section 610. The section states that a debtor needs to provide identification to others when aiming to get one's report.

Section 611

Section 611 discusses the points of how an investigation can take place in the event that there is a dispute over how accurate the report might be. The investigation can include:

- A full investigation must be instigated in the event there is a problem found on a report. This includes a review of where the problem originated.

- A notice must be provided to the person who is asking for information on the item in question. The notice can be provided to let the person know about the problem and what needs to be done to resolve the issue in question.

- A notice of determination must be provided when it is found that there is indeed an error that has to be resolved. The notice will identify problems with one's account and what needs to be done to correct the issues.

- When something cannot be confirmed, a notice is sent to the debtor about the situation and what can be done to resolve the issue in question.

Section 613

Employment information is the main focus of Section 613. The section concentrates mainly on reporting details about employment and credit. When an employer reviews a person's credit report, the employer must be able to identify vital details surrounding the specific types of debts one has. Specifically, the employer is entitled to review the public records on someone's account if there are any. The employer may use this information in identifying cases where the data could impair one's ability to manage finances responsibly.

Section 618

Section 618 states that while you can bring legal action to a court in the event that a bureau does not respond to your request or is not treating you fairly, you must also do so within a certain time period. Section 618 specifically says the following:

- You can have the dispute sent to a court within two years after the date of the discovery that the other party was liable of wrong-doing.

- You can have the dispute sent to a court within five years after the violation occurs.

Section 619

Section 619 protects people from having their identities duplicated through such checks. The law states that anyone who obtains information from a reporting group under false pretenses can be fined. A person may also be sent to jail for up to two years in some of the most extreme cases.

You can visit the FCRA website at ftc.gov to get a full copy of the FCRA and to see all the details on these sections and all the many others that might make an impact on your credit scores.

Chapter 16 – The Use of Section 809

Section 809 refers to the validation of debts. This refers to details of the debts that are listed under your name. It will be easier for your debts to be challenged if those debts cannot be validated.

Section 809 concentrates on how a creditor might try to demand certain debts to be paid by you. These include debts that you might have had listed on your credit report. You can use Section 809 in the event that you know those debts are not yours and cannot be validated.

The Validation Period

An important aspect of Section 809 is the debt verification period that has to be followed. The period refers to the time period when someone can list debts and confirm that they exist.

A debt collector should provide you with details of your debts within five days after contacting you about details of how much you owe and to whom.

Section 809 requires the creditor to state that you have the right to dispute the debt if you feel that it is unwarranted or you have already paid the debt. You have the right to dispute the debt within 30 days after the notice is sent to you.

You have to respond in writing to deny the debts that are on your report and/or to have the debts removed.

Sending a Request For Validation

You can request for a validation of the debt in question within the thirty-day period of receiving notice from a collector. You have many options to consider at this point:

1. You can dispute a certain value of the debt. There might be times when you are asked to retire the entire debt or maybe only a portion of your debt.

2. You can also request information on the identity of the original creditor.

3. The issue you have surrounding the credit and how it is being managed can be discussed in detail. You should explain why you feel the debt should be removed from your name.

The collector will not be able to demand funds from you until after the request is sent and received. You can use this point to see that you will not be hassled or pressured in any way.

You should use the same certified mail process that you used in a Section 609 process. You should also write the letter by hand and provide the appropriate items to confirm your identity.

What to Expect From the Response

The response from the collector regarding your Section 809 request should include the following:

- Proof that you own the debt

- Information about the original creditor

- Documentation proving that you owe the creditor

You have to ensure that you have proof that you paid off a debt or that you do not owe the debt. Your collector will surely have information indicating your debt. Therefore, you will have to do your own research on your credit to see what you deem is correct or what has been fabricated.

The collector will have up to 30 days to let you know that there are debts that need to be collected. The timeframe suggests that you must get the issue resolved by someone or else the debt cannot be removed. Specifically, the debt can be removed if the collector cannot get the proper data about your debt. This absolves you of that debt.

Section 809 will only work for your credit repairs if you are absolutely certain that you can get the problem in question resolved.

Could You Be Sued?

By working with Section 809, you can be assured no one will try to sue you to collect debts. This ensures your credit report will not be at risk of more damages. The fact that the creditor cannot collect debts from you at this point will be critical to ensure that a lawsuit will not occur.

A collector can only sue you if they confirmed the debt that you owe. If the collector cannot confirm it, that debt will be removed from your credit profile and that collector will no longer have the ability to sue you.

You can contact the FTC in the event that a collector tries to sue you beforehand. The collector will not be able to sue you until after the debt is confirmed.

Chapter 17 – Issuing a Consumer Statement

A consumer statement is very brief - only a hundred words in length. It will be added to your credit report. You can use this to explain a bad mark on your credit report if you wish. This could help you explain your side of the story.

The consumer statement is in accordance with the Fair Credit Reporting Act. The Act states that you have the right to add a statement up to a hundred words in length on any item that might be on your credit report.

This can be used if you have found something on your credit report that you have tried to dispute in the past but had been rejected. The dispute might have failed because the creditor or bureau had enough information to confirm the case.

You might use this to explain that there was a background issue surrounding the problem. You might state that you had lost your job and could not cover a certain debt. Maybe you might state that something happened that caused you to owe something but you did not have any actual liability. In short, you have the opportunity to state that there is a legitimate reason why you were unable to pay off certain debts.

Initially, you might feel comfortable having this recorded on your credit report. You may feel that your statement will be a sufficient explanation, but the truth is that it might do more harm to your credit than good.

There are a few problems that should be noticed when it comes to such a report:

1. This is not necessarily going to impact your credit score.

2. This is not going to cause an expense to decline either. That is, the value of the issue at hand will stay the same throughout the life of your credit report.

3. The statement may do more to draw attention to certain negative things on your report.

By adding such a statement, you are making it possible for employers, creditors, and other groups to pay more attention to the issue. You are not necessarily telling such a group that there was a problem that you were trying to resolve. Rather, you are simply drawing attention to the fact that you had that problem to begin with.

Therefore, the best thing to do with regards to a consumer statement is to avoid adding it in the first place. This is not necessarily going to do much for the credit repair process other than making one's credit report look worse by drawing attention to something negative.

If you have such a statement on your report and want it removed you must send a letter to the bureau in question and state the information on your account and request the statement be removed.

There is not much that you can do if the bureau is unable to remove the statement. You would have to wait for the item on your report to be dropped before you can get the statement removed from your report. This just makes it all the more important for you to avoid having any statements like this on your report.

Chapter 18 – Public Records on Your Report

Public records are reports that are more harmful to your credit and may stay on your credit report much longer than anything else that can be listed.

Your credit report covers what you have been doing lately with your money and much of what you have done in recent time. This is especially if you have been mentioned in certain public records that keep you from being fully trustworthy with regards to your money.

The public records section of your credit report will provide many details on what you have gone through in recent time that has shown you might be a dangerous borrower. Naturally, the best credit is one that has nothing in the public records section.

You may encounter one of these various records if you are not careful with your finances.

Bankruptcy – Chapter 7 and Chapter 13

By declaring bankruptcy, you are stating that you are unable to cover your debts as they are. This would result in a reorganization of your debts or a liquidation of assets. A bankruptcy is the most significant of the public records that might damage your credit rating.

Chapter 7 Bankruptcy: This occurs when your unsecured debts are cleared without having to pay them back through a plan. This works mainly for those with low incomes who have very few assets.

A Chapter 7 filing will hurt your credit rating more than anything else. The filing will stay on your credit report for ten years after you have filed for bankruptcy. The reason for this is that you have not paid off any of your debts. This makes it all the more important for you to devise a plan for managing your debts.

Chapter 13 Bankruptcy: You are reorganizing the plans you have for paying off your debts. You may use this to catch up on payments if you have the money to cover your debts. You would have to make monthly payments to your trustee to ensure that you get those old debts covered as soon as possible.

Your Chapter 13 filing will be removed seven years after it was issued. This is provided that you went through all the payments for the filing. The seven-year timeframe is used because you are at least covering some of the debts that you owe.

The impact on your credit report from a Chapter 13 filing may be minimal if enough time has passed between when it was filed and that seven-year period. This is provided that the debts involved within the period are covered accordingly.

Chapter 13 policy is clearly much easier for you to manage based on the impact on your credit rating.

You have to be aware of the problems you are entering into when you declare a bankruptcy as your finances will become much harder for you to manage.

Civil Judgment

A civil judgment is a case where you would have to pay someone a certain amount of money because of a court order. This may be the result of a lawsuit or other liability-related concern. Simply put, you will be subjected to a civil judgment if someone brings you to court and you lose the case.

A civil judgment will appear on your credit report for seven years after it was made.

Tax Liens

A tax lien is another issue that may stay on your credit report for years after it is filed. A lien is filed against you by the government in cases where you do not pay your taxes. You must pay your taxes regularly or else you might be at risk of having negative reports appear on your credit rating.

A tax lien can stay on your credit report for years, but the amount of time they will stay there will vary based on whether or not you have paid off the taxes in question. You could have a lien stay on your credit report for up to fifteen years if you do not pay those taxes accordingly.

A paid tax lien will stay on your report for seven years after the lien has been paid off.

How Can You Resolve These Issues?

The most common way for you to handle these problems to repair your credit is through simple time and effort. The court records that list many of these things that have taken place are going to be extremely difficult for you to debate or dispute.

There is always that chance that some error might be found in this section of your report. Refer to the chapter on managing disputes on your credit report for more details on this point.

Of course, Section 609 can be considered for getting these things off your report. As useful as Section 609 can be, the problem is that the courts that handled these public records will surely have all the data on your case on hand.

What If Judgments and Liens Were Discharged?

Even after the time period for one of these public records has passed, you may still notice that it is listed on your credit report. The record may also say that the record was discharged or paid off. Not everyone will have these reports on their accounts after they are paid off or discharged. Sometimes you might find the entire section is empty. It sometimes takes some time for the discharge to show up as resolved on your credit report.

Chapter 19 – Good vs. Bad Debts

You have to look at the types of debts you have and what needs to be covered first. Part of this includes looking at the good debts that you have. Owing good debts will not be as harmful to your credit report as the bad debts. You would have to pay them off just like you would do with every other debt. However, those good debts are not ones that you have to pay off right away.

You must resolve the bad debts including the unsecured debts before you consider paying off the good debts if possible. Having a credit report that includes more good debts than bad debts is always good.

Good Debt

A good debt is one that helps you build the assets you have. With good debt, you are producing income while also expanding upon your net worth.

There are many types of good debts:

1. Real Estate Investments

Real estate investments include not only any properties you live in but also your business properties or any properties around the world that you have a stake in. People often use these real estate properties for years before they sell them, possibly at a profit.

Of course, many people may rent out those properties as a means of making an income. This especially since the home rental and vacation rental industry has been blossoming. The expenses associated with these real estate investments often include mortgage payments, homeowners' insurance costs, and maintenance charges.

2. Investments

Investments include many debts relating to stocks, commodities, currencies, bonds, precious metals, futures, and many other things you might be interested in. These investments can produce great profits over time, but they may also be risky. Some investments may be even riskier than others, particularly alternative investments that are not as widely followed as other options.

You might contribute a certain amount of money to an IRA every year. The thousands of dollars you spend on this investment is a good debt because you are working to get your IRA to grow in value over time.

3. Small Business Functions

The expenses associated with owning and operating a business can be high and may include charges relating to renting a property, maintaining an inventory, marketing, managing employees, and so forth. The charges associated with running a small business is interpreted as good debts.

4. Educational Expenses

Educational expenses involved with attending college or receiving training to earn a degree, certification are considered good debts because they will help you to potentially earn even more money through the newfound credentials or experience.

These good debts still need to be paid off like with any other debt, but not as quickly as bad debts.

Risks of Good Debts

Although the good debts that you come across are beneficial, there are plenty of concerns that should be noticed.

- The high costs of a real estate investment could be too high when the expenses associated with running it are considered. The fact that these will continue throughout the life of your investment might prove to be a challenge to manage.

- There is a chance that your stock investments, real estate investments might lose value. The markets for all of these are unpredictable and challenging.

- Every small business runs the same risk of failure as a large business.

- Increasing your education might not work as well as you might wish due to a difficult job market, changes in trends, difficulties with relocating, and so forth.

You have to look at what you're going to get out any good debt to know how it will be a financial benefit to you.

Bad Debts

Bad debts are the debts that need to be paid off first. You must make sure they are resolved first as they will do more to hurt your credit rating. The following are examples of bad debts:

1. Consumable Goods

These are best described as the debts incurred on your credit and charge cards. The biggest problem with the debts that involve consumable goods is that are not going to last forever, hence the name.

It should also be noted that the values of consumable goods are often considered to be about half of what was paid for them. Clothes wear out and food gets eaten, for instance.

2. Credit Card Debts

Consumable goods can make up a sizable portion of your credit card debts. Anything that you put on your credit cards can be bad debts. This is due to how credit card debts are typically unsecured. The interest rates on credit cards are often much higher than other loans.

3. Cars

Most people need a car to get around, especially if you have a job that requires you to travel. The problem is that a car can be seen as a bad debt for the following reasons:

- The interest charges on a car loan can be high. This is assuming you have a car loan.

- Insurance costs can be rather high. You cannot go without car insurance as it is required by law. If you get into an accident or you encounter some trouble like a traffic violation while on the road, your insurance premiums can be affected.

- Oil, gas, tires, and general maintenance can be a burden.

- Your car's value will always depreciate. Depreciation begins immediately after you buy the car.

Paying off the entire car loan is clearly the best idea to avoid interest charges. You could always consider a less costly used vehicle as the depreciation will be significantly lower.

Are These Good or Bad?

This next section is devoted to certain debts that might be either good or bad. You might find that they are useful for many things in your life, but that does not mean each of them is a necessity.

1. Investment Borrowing

You might need to borrow some money to purchase an investment. The borrowing process requires leverage. This occurs when you are borrowing money with the intention of investing that money. The leveraged money will be borrowed with a low rate of interest. Meanwhile, the money will be invested in something with the potential of it having a higher rate of return.

This could be interesting for your investments, but there is the chance that your investment will drop in value, although that can be said for just about anything you might invest in.

2. Consolidation Loans

A consolidation loan takes many debts you have and combines them into one loan. This may include a lower interest rate. Consolidation will be discussed later in this guide.

3. Credit Card Rewards

One of the top reasons why so many people open credit card accounts is because of the rewards. From frequent flyer miles to cash back offers, there are many things that you might come across when getting a credit card to work for you.

That does not mean every credit card is going to be worthwhile. You should consider the risks associated with the credit card you are going to use. More importantly, you have to consider how often you plan to use the card.

The main goal for your debts is to make sure the bad ones are paid off first.

Chapter 20 – Your Credit Card Purchases Matter

Your credit card will have a certain limit attached to it. It is information that you should have been given when you first got the card. In most cases, you might assume that you're going to keep well below the limit of your card. There is always a chance that your purchase might come close to maxing out your card.

For instance, you might buy a new refrigerator for your home. A refrigerator can cost thousands of dollars and that one purchase could put your card near or at the limit. There is a chance that the charge you put on your credit card will directly influence your ability to pay off the balance.

Your Credit Can Be Hurt by a Big Purchase

It is sensible that you would want to buy something with a credit card. You might feel that you are covering the entire cost of your transaction all at once and that you can pay off what is owed soon. The fact is that a large purchase on a credit card might be too hard for you to cover.

There are many reasons why your credit may be harmed when you make a large purchase:

1. You are using more of your credit than necessary.

A massive credit card purchase can get close to the spending limit of that card. For instance, you might have a credit limit of $5,000 on your card and consider purchasing a refrigerator worth $3,500. In this example, you would use 70 percent of your credit on one purchase.

2. You could be at risk of overspending on your card.

That massive purchase could be forgotten and you would continue to spend on the card. At this juncture, you are at risk of spending more money on your card than what is allowed.

By going over, you are showing that you have no concern over your credit limit. In addition, you would be subjected to a substantial fine on your card if you go over the limit.

3. It could be hard for you to pay off the total debt you have incurred on your card.

The more you put on your credit card, the more interest is owed. This would make your credit situation worse.

All of these issues can add up and make it harder to get your credit cards paid off, not to mention make it harder for you to get a good deal on whatever it is you are buying.

What to Consider

The threats that you will put upon your credit may be significant if you spend too much on your card. The damage to your credit could be significant because of the extra expenses and other problems. However, you do not have to fall into that hole of spending more than what you can afford.

There are several things to consider when managing your credit card with larger purchases in mind:

1. Avoid getting close to your credit limit on a card.

Have a goal to spend less than 60 to 70 percent of the credit limit on your card if possible. This should be enough to keep your charge card totals manageable. Having some credit open is vital. Not having enough on your card will keep you from being trusted as someone who can manage credit accordingly.

2. Review how much time you are spending between major purchases.

You do not want to add massive purchases to your credit card too often. Keep a few weeks or months in between those purchases.

3. Decide before you make a certain purchase if you really need it or if you can purchase a cheaper item.

Be cautious as you work with credit card purchases. Being responsible for getting your credit card transactions handled is vital for helping you to keep your credit under control. Adding too much onto your credit card could be dangerous to your credit rating.

Chapter 21 – The Truth About Credit Card Limits

When you apply for a credit card or other type of payment card, you will be subjected to a limit. The limit is designed to ensure that you do not go over a certain amount on your card. A creditor will impose a limit based on your history to ensure that the creditor will not be at risk of losing money to someone who might be a risk.

Your credit card limit is critical to your credit history and report. You need to have a high limit to ensure that you can have a better rating and you will have more spending power to work with. You must still avoid charging up to that limit or else you might be seen as a high-risk client, thus causing your score to go down some more.

What Determines Your Credit Card Limit?

There are many things that will determine your credit limit.

1. Your Credit Score

Your credit score is the most basic point that will determine what your credit rating will be. You will get a higher credit limit if your score is greater.

2. Your Income

Although your credit score will determine your credit limit, it is even more important that you can show that you have sufficient income to pay off that credit. Your income would be reviewed based on your tax returns and other details.

You would have to provide information on your income when applying for a card. This would be compared with information on your tax returns. When the credit card company notices your income, that group will determine a proper value for your credit based on what you can afford to pay off within a certain amount of time.

3. Your Repayment History

Your ability to pay off the card can influence what a creditor might consider after you have had the card for a period of time. The creditor might feel that you are indeed capable of paying off your debts on-time, thus allowing that creditor to give you a higher credit limit. This, in turn, improves upon your credit score even more.

4. Debt to Income Ratio

Your debt to income ratio refers to how much income you have versus the debts you accumulate. When you have more income and less debt, you are showing to a credit card company that you can manage your credit well.

A good thing about your credit limit is that your creditor might take a look at your account on occasion to see that it works well. You might be able to get an increase after a regular check. Each card team will look at accounts at different times. A group might review accounts every six to twelve months, but others might wait a little longer.

No-Limit Cards Are False

When looking for a credit card, you might see something like a no-limit credit card. This gives the impression that you can spend as much on that card as you want.

Let's be realistic. Do you genuinely believe that someone would give you a no-limit card that will provide you with all the spending power you have ever wanted? There's no way that this would happen. The creditor would be at risk of letting you buy literally anything you want without any real consequences involved.

So, what is a no-limit card? A no-limit card is actually one that says there are no preset limits on the card. The limit is based on your spending habits. That total could be flexible depending on what you spend on it. There is a chance that the limit could be increased, but the good news is that the odds of the limit decreasing will be extremely minimal.

This is a trick that many credit card companies will use. They will market themselves as offering no-limit cards, but those cards will have real limits. They will just vary based on one's use. The card company will hide information about those limits in the fine print of the application.

Be aware of this when finding a good card that works for you and has a sensible limit. It might be easy for you to find a great deal on a card if you are careful and ask questions.

What You Can Do to Improve Your Credit Limit

It is clear that you should charge close to your credit limit when using your card or else your credit limit will be at risk. If you increase that credit limit over time, it becomes a little easier for you to spend more money without going over that limit. It is better to have a limit of $5,000 while spending up to $2,500 on it than it is to have a limit of $3,000. Besides, having a higher limit shows that you are responsible with your money.

There are many things that can be done to increase your credit limit:

1. Make sure you make your payments regularly and on-time.

This is the most important point as a few missed payments will surely ruin your credit score.

2. Use your line of credit for a longer period of time.

Creditors typically provide long-term clients with better credit limits. They do this as a means of rewarding people for their loyalty.

3. Avoid adding more onto your card than necessary.

Keep the balance owed under the 50% of your credit limit.

4. Contact the creditor after a while to see if you can get a higher credit limit.

Sometimes a credit card company will automatically provide you with a higher credit limit if you have done well enough with your existing one. This is not always the case, but it is a simple convenience that you will enjoy.

Ask For an Increase on Your Credit Limit

Getting a higher credit limit is a good way to help you repair your credit score. Many credit card companies are willing to give you a higher limit.

What to Consider Before Asking

Start your search for a higher credit by taking a look at your credit situation first.

1. Check on your credit score first.

It will be easier to get an increase on your credit limit if your credit score has improved recently.

2. Think about why you need a higher credit limit.

You might have to explain to the creditor why you want to increase your credit limit.

3. Think about how much credit you really need.

You should be realistic when it comes to your request for an added credit limit. Avoid asking for a huge increase.

The Process of Asking

There are a few steps that can be used when asking for a better credit limit:

1. Check on how you can contact the credit card company. You might go online, but you could also possibly send a request by mail.

2. Discuss your history of using your card.

Talk about as many details on your card as possible. Describe how long you have had the card and how much time you have spent paying it off. Be sure to talk about your payment plans and that you have not gone beyond your limit.

3. Explain your finances if possible.

You might mention that your income has increased dramatically recently. Do not mention other debts that you have.

4. Be direct and explain why you need to increase your credit limit.

Be specific about what you plan on purchasing.

5. Never Act desperate when requesting the credit increase.

6. Don't expect an immediate response.

Be willing to spend a bit of time waiting to see if you will get a higher credit limit. The credit card company receives many requests, so be patient.

Be Aware of the Credit Check

Don't forget the credit check is a full view of your credit report. The credit check will cost a few points off your credit score, but it won't be much.

When Should You Apply For an Increase?

Do not bother asking for an increased limit for a new card. Credit card companies want to ensure that the people who use their cards make regular and on-time payments and work toward paying them off over a longer period of time. Do not ask for an increase on a card that is less than six months to a year old.

Can You Apply For a Card With a Higher Limit?

You have the option to apply for a new credit card that has a higher limit. That is not necessarily the best thing to do to improve your credit rating. There are many problems associated with doing this as they can impact your credit score:

- This would require another inquiry on your credit report, thus costing points on your rating.

- The fees associated with some high-limit cards may be too high.

You would have to pay annual fees on some of these cards. Sometimes a company might provide you with a fee-free service for the first year, but that might be to mask the high value of the fee after that year is up. Don't forget about the interest rates; those fancy cards might come with very high rates due to their limits being high. These high rates are to offset the risks associated.

- Many groups that offer high-limit cards are extremely selective about choosing their applicants.

- You might also be subjected to fees even when you do not use the card.

The fees in question might be small in value, but they can add up if you ignore your card. Many high-end companies, particularly luxury-oriented groups like American Express, might cause you to spend more than needed on your account.

Having a higher limit will increase your credit rating, but you must be aware of how you are spending money surrounding that limit.

Chapter 22 – Using the Credit Card Act to Your Advantage

The Credit Card Act is a law that was passed in 2009 and went into action in 2010. The Credit Card Accountability, Responsibility, and Disclosure Act was designed to ensure that credit card companies are direct and truthful with their clients.

When building credit, you should take advantage of how the Credit Card Act works. You may use the Act to help you to uncover issues with your card, which could potentially reduce the amount of money you owe on your card.

This chapter concentrates on how you can use the Credit Card Act to your advantage when managing your credit card debts. The points in the Act are designed to protect people from predatory credit card companies, but they will also help you devise a good plan to have your credit card debts paid.

Rate Increase Terms

A credit card issuer cannot raise the rate on your balance unless it was a promotional rate that has expired. Look at any promotional rates on your card and the length of time they are in force. Determine the regular rate after the promotional rate expires.

However, the credit card group has the right to increase the rate on your card after giving you 45 days' notice.

What can you do in the event you need help paying off an overdue debt? Let's suppose that you are 60 days or more late on making payments on your card. If you make on-time payments for six months or more, your rate will go back to whatever the default might be for the card. This provides you with the opportunity to cover your debts within a sensible time.

The interest that you will be charged will decline.

There are a few additional points about this rule on the Act to consider:

- A credit card cannot raise the rate on a card within the first year after the card has been issued.

- A promotional rate on a new card must in effect for at least the first six months.

- A rate can be raised in the event of a 60-day delinquency or when a card plan changes.

Expect to be given proper notice when the rate changes. This is even in cases where the rate decreases. The client must be made aware of the changes.

Increased Timeframe for Rate Hikes

As mentioned just a moment ago, the Credit Card Act states that the company must remind its clients with 45 days' notice about any changes in a rate. The timeframe before the Act was passed was only 15 days.

There are a few problems that must be noticed:

- Credit limit changes are not subjected to such advance notices. These include cases where a credit limit would decline. An exception may be made if the decline could potentially trigger an overcharge fee unless it is paid off.

- An increase in the rate can be as high as the credit card company wants it to be. This could be twice the value depending on what the card company sees fit.

- People are not able to challenge points relating to rate changes. The rate changes used on cards often work through an entire borrowing network, and the terms can be significantly varied.

Fee Rules

You might be able to get some of the fees on your card waived if they are issued against the standards of the Credit Card Act. You could refer to the Act when contesting a fee on your card if you have to.

The Act states that a credit card issuer cannot charge over-limit fees unless a cardholder allows the creditor to support over-limit transactions. That is, a person might be able to get a limit on the card to ensure that a transaction does not move forward if the value is higher than the limit in question.

What makes this valuable is that the issuer cannot charge a person more than one over-limit fee during the course of a billing cycle.

A customer cannot be charged a fee due to that person working to pay off a card online or by phone. Some companies have added extra fees for online and phone transactions just to raise extra funds. You could contest any of these fees.

In addition, fees on cards for people with poor credit ratings are limited. After a person's first year with one of these low-value cards, the non-penalty fees involved with a card cannot be more than 25 percent of whatever the credit limit may be. Consult the credit company about any fees that go beyond that total. The company would have to reimburse any of these fees due to the added costs involved in the process.

No Double-Cycle Billing

Double-cycle billing is a problematic concern that many card issuers use just to gather more money from cardholders. A company will calculate the interest to be charged within a certain billing period. The average daily balance of a card in the current billing cycle is calculated alongside the daily balance average from the last cycle.

The double-cycle billing is used to get a card company to manage finance charges through an unfair practice. An issuer might charge interest in not only the debts one has now but also whatever debts that person owed in the past.

To identify cases where double-cycle billing occurs:

1. Review your total balance on your card and look at how the interest on your card is calculated based on that total.

2. Determine how much you owed in interest on the last payment that you made.

3. Analyze the added interest charges from the last month compared with what is on your present statement. This works especially if the balance on your card in the current month is less than what you had a month earlier.

4. Consult the credit card company about the charges in question. The company should notice that it has double-billed you and reduce the amount owing.

The process of double-billing is so intricate that it is easy for groups to hide their content from you. More importantly, it might be easy for a group to get away with double-billing because so many people might assume the process entails just having duplicate charges on one's account.

Knowing how to identify double-billing is critical for reducing the amount of money you would have to spend on your card. Always keep careful records of your credit cards payments as you aim to pay them off and figure out if you are paying more in interest than necessary.

Review How Payments Are Moved

Before the Credit Card Act was passed, card companies could direct payments toward the card with the lowest rate. Card companies often did this keep the balances on the higher rate cards from being reduced, thus charging more interest on that particular card.

The Credit Card Act states that you need to be given the ability to have your card payments go to the right cards. Above-minimum payments must go to the card balance that has the highest interest rate. This ensures that you have an easier time with paying off bills without worrying about the interest rate on the card being impacted by not having a payment recorded.

Contact the card company if you notice the higher interest charge not covered properly.

Payment Time

A card company has to send you a statement 21 days before your payment is due. This also helps to know when a billing cycle ends and when the next one will start.

Before the Act was passed, the timeframe was only 14 days.

This part of the Act does not require too much work on your end. Having enough warning is useful for noticing when a payment has to be made.

Note when the billing period ends and when the next one starts. You can review the interest charges relating to each billing period to see how the billing works. You can use this to determine you are being double-billed.

The Credit Card Act is a helpful policy that assists people to ensure that they will not be subjected to extreme charges or abuses from credit card companies.

Chapter 23 – Which Credit Card Should You Pay Off First?

How many credit cards are you trying to pay off? It's perfectly understandable if you have several cards that need to be covered. After all, the average person in the United States more than likely has several different types of cards.

Experian found in a 2015 study that an average American has about 2.25 credit cards. Anyone could get into trouble by forgetting about certain cards or how those cards are to be used.

The fact is people often get multiple credit cards for many reasons. Some people might use different cards for specific types of purchases. Others might have cards that are reserved specifically for work-related expenses.

Many people are willing to sign up for credit cards because of the bonuses that they offer. For instance, many airlines have credit cards where a cardholder can earn special reward points that go toward free air travel.

Whatever the case may be, people are often willing to have many credit cards. They feel that each of the cards they use will have specific benefits.

It becomes very easy for people to forget to pay off certain cards. They will struggle to keep their cards managed and therefore start to owe more money on certain cards due to interest rates, late fees, and other charges. The charges can add up.

You will have to pay off certain cards first before all others. There are a few points you can consider when figuring out which cards are to be paid off first.

What Is the Interest Rate?

Look at what the interest rates of each card and see which ones are the highest. The ones with the highest rates are always best to pay off first. A card with a 15% rate is going to become harder to pay off than one with an 8% rate.

How Late is the Payment?

You cannot afford to be too overdue on your payments. Anything that causes you to be significantly overdue could hurt your credit rating. Remember that TransUnion uses those colored boxes to show how far in arrears you are. Those whose payments are the most overdue will be at a greater risk.

Specifically, you could have more harm done to your credit rating if you have debts that are far in arrears. These include debts that are so in arrears that a creditor might try to take you to court to get those debts paid off sooner.

The key is to pay off the credit cards that you owe old debts on first. Getting those charges covered sooner is vital.

You should also look at how often you are late making credit card payments. There are often times when you might be late too often and this will damage your credit rating.

What Fees Are Being Charged?

The fees associated with your credit card should be checked. The fees might be higher than the added interest charges that you might be struggling with. The fees could be charged because of many things like:

- How much money is owed

- How long you have owed that money

- Any specific types of debts you have on your credit line

- Whether you have managed to handle minimum payments

Check on the terms of your credit to see what fees are due when you do not pay off what you owe. You might expect to find expensive fees that are worth more than the interest totals. The cards with the highest fees might need to be paid off first.

A Simple Strategy

Here are some steps you can use for getting your cards paid:

1. Start by making payments on the debts that are in the greatest arrears. These include the debts that are the most overdue as well as anything that causes you to pay late fees.

2. Look at the fees and interest charges on your cards. Pay on the cards that have the highest fees and charges first.

3. You can concentrate on the small-value cards later on.

4. You should also look at a maximum time frame with which you can afford to be late on payments. Avoid going beyond that time frame.

You must look into each of the cards you have when deciding how you are going to pay them off.

Later in this guide, you will learn about strategies involving paying off the cards that have the most value on them first as well as another strategy for paying off the smallest balances first.

Chapter 24 – Using the Fair Credit Billing Act

Imagine that you have been charged for something that you never expected to come across. This could hurt your ability to handle your credit debts because you are being forced into paying for something that you never got or did not ask for. This can be a tough hassle, but you do not have to struggle with an unfair billing process if you use the Fair Credit Billing Act to your advantage.

The Fair Credit Billing Act or FCBA is a law that can be utilized to help you with managing the charges that you could be subjected to. Knowing how to make this work for you can help you with doing more for getting a charge covered accordingly.

The FCBA is a part of the Truth in Lending Act that was passed in 1974. The Act is designed to keep people from being subjected to unfair billing practices. This includes managing billing errors in credit card accounts among others that a person might be subjected to.

Common Errors

Some of the errors that may be made that are against the Fair Credit Billing Act include the following:

- Charges that a customer did not actually make.

- Charges might be calculated using the wrong totals.

- The charges on a bill might be for goods or services that a person never received.

- The charges may be for goods that someone agreed to but never received.

- Any goods that were damaged in the delivery process should not be included in one's account. Sometimes a bill might include charges for those items.

- A credit group may fail to recognize the payments that were made to one's account.

These errors are not produced because someone might have been abusive or neglectful. It is often a simple error.

Using the FCBA to Your Advantage

A few things can be done to help you get the FCBA to work for you:

1. Send a letter to the creditor that has listed the incorrect information on your account.

Look for the billing inquiry address. You would have to use this instead of the one that you regularly send your payments to. Be sure to do this within 60 days of the statement date.

Use an overnight mail service.

You might have the right to file a dispute online, but this might be costly. Going online to handle an FCBA-related dispute might cause you to waive your rights under the law.

Using the phone to file a complaint or dispute is not recommended. Phone-related inquiries are not protected under the law.

2. Wait to see that the creditor has accepted your letter.

The creditor needs to send you a response within 30 days stating that the group has received your letter.

3. The creditor has up to 90 days to make the correction or to explain why they cannot do so.

4. You will have the right to ask for the creditor's documents stating that there is no error or that the error cannot be removed.

You might have the option to contact the Federal Trade Commission in the event that the creditor in question is refusing to help you. The FTC is responsible for administering the law.

You can file a lawsuit against the creditor if the item in question is not removed. This could take an extended period of time and would work the same way as dealing with the FCRA. However, you have the ability to recover an extensive amount of money if the suit is successful. You can recover the damages to your account plus twice whatever the charges were and all attorney fees and other costs associated with the case.

The legal option would work best in cases where the debts in question are very high.

An FCBA Loophole

One useful loophole relating to the FCBA that you can use focuses on the quality of the transaction in question. This can be used if the transaction that you are disputing is in your home state or within a hundred miles of your home address and the total value of the issue is greater than $50.

You must discuss the product or service that you ordered. This might include a dispute over the quality of the item in question. You might explain that whatever you use was not good enough or that it failed to work. Your request for reviewing the billing issue should be reasonable and sensible.

You have to talk to the vendor in question about resolving the bill by refunding the charge provided you either return the product or stop using the service.

This loophole is not always going to work, but it might be valuable in cases where you have a large debt to cover but the product or service was not of the best quality.

Additional Points About the FCBA

There are a few extra considerations relating to the FCBA that should be explored just as well when getting the situation under control:

- Any billing statements relating to what you owe should be sent to you at least fourteen days before your payment is due.

- A grace period should be provided.

- A credit card company cannot prevent merchants from being able to pay with cash or check.

- Any bank that reports payments as being delinquent should also report cases where charges may be disputed.

- Money in a person's checking or savings account with a bank or credit union cannot be used to pay off a credit account that is overdue.

You might be able to dispute a situation with your creditor if any of these considerations surrounding the FCBA are violated. You have to write a letter to the creditor discussing that the violation took place and offer enough proof about the situation. This may help you dramatically reduce some of the credit card debts that you have.

The FCBA should help you get your credit card charges managed and ensure you can dispute anything that might be charged on your card in error. Be certain you have enough details and proof to back your claims.

Chapter 25 – The Truth in Lending Act

A valuable law that cannot be ignored when it comes to your finances is the Truth in Lending Act. The TILA was passed in 1968 as a law to help people manage consumer credit functions responsibly. The TILA focuses mainly on terms and costs associated with financial services.

This Act may be used to repair credit functions and to help people understand the service they are being offered. A person could use the Act to dispute any actions that a creditor takes, thus dramatically reducing the debts or charges. This may also help reduce the damages that may be found on one's credit report.

The TILA concentrates on the terms and costs of financial services while ensuring that all groups use the same standards to review finance charges. People can shop for the best possible rates when looking for lines of credit or other services.

A lender must provide you with various details surrounding your investments:

- The cost associated with your loan should be explained based on how much money you are able to borrow.

There are limits as to how much you can borrow. The total you may actually be able to borrow may vary based on your credit rating.

- All rates on loans should be discussed.

The rate can include not only the basic rate for a loan but also any promotional or introductory rates plus changes that might happen on the loan. The rate that you would pay may vary based on your credit history and whatever a lender might determine is appropriate.

- Any fees that you might be charged must be explained.

Fees may include late charges, early repayment totals, and anything else that might be added to the loan.

What is even more important about the Truth in Lending Act is that you have the right of rescission when getting in or out of a loan. This means that you can opt out of a loan within three days. You are given the right to reconsider the loan or other investment you are negotiating.

The right of rescission gives you time to withdraw your application for a loan that you might have been forced into due to high-pressure sales tactics. Many people are pressured into agreeing to such loans because of high-stress tactics used by various salesmen.

What If a Violation Occurs?

There is always a chance that a violation of the Act may take place. Such a violation would entitle you to collect money to help you manage your loan debt or to improve your credit rating.

TILA states that the proper disclosures should be provided to you at any time. If those disclosures are not provided and you are not given the help you need, you may file a dispute about the situation with the lender.

In the event that a violation of TILA occurs regarding your account, you must:

1. Consult the lender and ask for information surrounding the issue. Be sure to provide information on the TILA violation plus documentation that proves the situation.

2. Provide a letter regarding the concern to the billing inquiry website of the lender in question.

3. Allow the creditor to have enough time to review the report. You should give the creditor around 30 days or so to review the dispute.

4. You might also consider filing a suit with the lender if this does not work. You would have to contact a consumer attorney in the event that this does not work appropriately.

You should recover any charges that were sustained as a result of the lender's failure. Any statutory damages caused by the charges may also be covered. This should be about twice the finance charges, but there are limits. The statutory damages should be from $400 to $4,000 in accordance with the TILA standards.

The Truth in Lending Act is a simple law, but it is one that can be used to protect you. Be aware of how well the law works as you aim to get your expenses surrounding your loan managed. It could help you reduce what you owe and improve your credit rating.

Chapter 26 – The Fair Debt Collection Practices Act

Debt collectors are notorious for being difficult to work with. There is a law that works in the United States to ensure that any debts that do need to be collected can be handled appropriately. This law is the Fair Debt Collection Practices Act, and it focuses on helping people to ensure their debts are to be collected fairly.

The FDCPA is designed to ensure that people are protected from abusive credit collection practices.

The Act also provides you with the ability to receive all the information that you need to dispute some action of a creditor. The Act provides you with a solution for handling the debts that you have.

The main concept of the FDCPA is to help ensure that creditors will not engage in abusive practices. The Act limits how debtors are consulted, when they can be contacted, how often they can be contacted, etc. The details in the Act are extensive provide protection from any abusive or questionable actions that a creditor might engage in.

The Act keeps you from bearing with the intense stress that many creditors often try to impose. Creditors often try to ask more from their debtors than what they can handle.

What Is Prohibited?

You may be able to file a complaint in the event that the creditor in question engages in illegal actions. This could help you to get some of the debts or issues you have on your credit report removed as a means of reparations for any abuses you have been subjected to.

The prohibited actions that are listed in the FDCPA include the following:

- Debtors cannot be contacted outside of regular hours. In this case, debtors cannot be consulted after 9pm or before 8am.

- Debtors cannot be contacted if they have requested validations of their debts.

A validation refers to a case where someone is trying to confirm that there is an error on a credit report or on a financial account. The validation process may take some time, and until the process is complete, the creditor will not be able to contact the debtor.

- A creditor cannot contact someone when that person is working with an attorney to manage certain debt-related problems.

A request to cease communication with an attorney must be obeyed by a creditor.

- Repeated calling is also outlawed.

Repeated calling, in this case, refers to situations where a person is frequently abused and hassled by a creditor. This can include cases where someone is contacted multiple times a day. Many creditors try to harass or bother debtors in the hopes that they will pay; the Act prevents those groups from being able to do this without repercussions.

- Misrepresentation is also illegal.

Misrepresentation refers to cases where a creditor might try to use a disguise or alias to try and collect a debt. For instance, a creditor might try to disguise oneself as an attorney, police officer, or other authority. This is often done to try to frighten or intimidate people into paying their debts sooner.

- Creditors cannot contact debtors at their places of employment.

This is an abusive practice that entails trying to contact someone too often. It may reach the point of harassment.

- The threat of an arrest for not covering one's debts is prohibited.

- Abusive language or open hostility are prohibited in the collection process.

- A creditor cannot seek an unreasonable amount of money.

Creditors might try to demand payment in full of one's debts at once. This is illegal; a creditor must abide by the minimum payment standards and other rules for collecting the funds.

- The practice of posting false information on one's credit report is illegal. Any threats of completing this action are also illegal.

- Threats demanding payment to keep one's credit report from being harmed is illegal.

- Any interactions that a creditor has with third parties are to be restricted.

A creditor may talk with a debtor's spouse or attorney if needed. Other people associated with the debtor may be consulted with regards to location details or other identifying information. A creditor may not talk with other people associated with the debtor about any urgent issues. The debtor should only be consulted at a reasonable time and with enough time given to the debtor to make payments.

What the Creditor Must Do

While there are plenty of things that a creditor definitely has to avoid doing, but there are some things that the creditor must do:

- When the creditor contacts the debtor, the creditor must directly tell that debtor about the situation.

The creditor will identify itself as a debt collector and be open and truthful about the situation.

- The creditor must indicate who can be consulted for further details regarding a debt.

- A person's Section 809 rights should be explained.

Section 809 ensures a person can dispute the debt in question. The creditor may also talk with the debtor about what the person can do in regards to Section 809.

- The creditor needs to confirm that a certain form of debt is owed by the debtor.

A debtor can ask the creditor to provide confirmation of the debt.

What If a Creditor Contravenes the Act?

The Fair Debt Collection Practices Act is enforced to ensure creditors will be sensible and controlled when aiming to collect money from debtors. The law is enforced by the Federal Trade Commission and the Consumer Financial

Protection Bureau. A debtor can contact these entities in the event that a creditor violates the Act.

1. File a report with the CFPB or FTC when you notice that there are problems with the creditor's practice of contacting you.

You can talk with either group and give details about the actions that the group has engaged in. This works best if you can record calls or present abusive letters or emails that are consistently being sent out to you.

2. Give the organizations your data. The groups may consult the creditor to investigate further.

3. You should expect to a few weeks to receive a reply to your query.

You also have the option to file a lawsuit against the creditor. That process would take more time and effort and require an extensive amount of proof showing that there is something wrong with the collection process.

You may receive a sizable reward if you can prove that the creditor in question was being abusive and contravened the law. You may get a reward of up to $1,000 and have any negative points on your credit report or removed or added fees reversed. This could help you improve your credit rating and also cover the debts that you owe.

You could be at risk of losing more money if you are unsuccessful in proving your accusations. You may have to pay the creditor's legal fees if you are unsuccessful.

It should also be noted that the $1,000 total that you may collect is the maximum amount for which you are entitled.

This has been considered by consumer groups to be an unfair total and should be at least $4,000. However, it would be unwise to dispute the value of the award.

Chapter 27 – Managing a Balance Transfer on Credit Cards

You do not necessarily have to accept the same rate for each of the cards that you have. You might have debts on multiple credit cards.

A balance transfer is a solution you can use to consolidate your credit card-related issues. This is a process where you will move the debt on one credit card to another.

In a balance transfer, a credit card company will accept the balance owing on another credit card. The new company may charge a fee to accept that debt. The cardholder will then pay off that entire debt in full over time.

The goal is to consolidate your payments to make them easy to cover while possibly having a lower rate involved. This is a process that many credit card companies are willing to do.

You may be surprised at how many credit card companies are willing to accept these balance transfers. They know that by working with such transfers, they will make money on the interest charges.

How the Process Works

How to initiate a balance transfer:

1. First, you would have to request the transfer. This must work within the limits of the card company. Details on the process for managing the transfer will be covered later in this chapter.

2. The accepting credit card group would then send a request to the card company that is holding your balance and they would notify them of their intent to assume the balance.

3. You are then subjected to the terms of the new credit card company including the chances for a better interest rate or friendlier terms.

Why Complete a Balance Transfer?

There are many reasons why a balance transfer might be a good idea for you to consider when resolving your credit card-related issues:

- You could negotiate a lower interest rate.

In addition to a lower interest rate, you might be given a special introductory rate. This could be lower in value or even fully eliminated. Either way, the rate will work for your account for a certain period.

- It becomes easier for you to cover the debts at a time.

By having one payment to work with each month instead of paying on multiple cards, you will have a better chance to pay off your debts.

- You are showing a commitment to the process of paying off your debts.

Creditors want to see that you are putting in an effort toward managing your debts. By using a balance transfer, it indicates that you are attempting to resolve those debts as soon as possible.

What to Know About Balance Transfers Beforehand

There are some rules to follow when employing a balance transfer.

- Consider the fee to initiate a balance transfer.

A fee will be applied based on the total amount of money you are transferring. The fee will traditionally be 3 to 5 percent on average. For instance, a transfer of $4,000 with a 5% charge to it would involve a fee of $200 for the process. The fee is charged because the new credit card company will be accepting the added risk associated with the new debt.

You may get a certain amount of money transferred with no added fees or the first $500 may be transferred with no fees, for instance.

- Be sure the interest rate on the new card is appropriate.

You can potentially get a lower interest rate on your card balance after a transfer. This is a big part of why so many people complete balance transfers. They want to take advantage of those reduced interest rates. At the same time, you must make sure that it is not going to change or increase quickly.

- Determine the interest-free period for the balance transfer.

One of the most common reasons why people open credit cards is so they can transfer old debts onto a new card with little to no interest offered at the beginning. While this is valuable, you must determine how long that interest-free period is.

You would still have to make payments during that interest-free period. Failing to make a payment will result in that interest-free period ending prematurely requiring you to pay the regular interest rate.

- Review if your transfer balance can be covered by an interest-free period.

Your existing debts might not be covered as a part of the interest-free promotion. Make sure that the balance transferred is covered by an interest-free period.

- Watch for any credit-related limits that might be imposed as a result of the balance transfer process.

While this process is designed for credit repair, it might not be advantageous for you if you have a poor credit history. Many credit card companies are more likely to help people to transfer credit lines if they have good credit histories.

Shop around to see what groups will help you consolidate your debts. The key is to see that the transfer program you use is one you will benefit from and be one that you can qualify to use.

How to Complete a Balance Transfer

Here is an explanation of what you can do to complete a transfer.

1. Apply for a new credit card.

The best card to choose should be one that has a rate you can afford. It is best to look for something with zero interest and no fees involved.

2. Review the account information for whatever it is you want to transfer your funds from.

Decide the amount of money you want to transfer. You don't necessarily have to transfer debts from all your cards. You can choose the amount you want to be transferred to the new card.

3. Contact the customer service team of the new credit card company and give them the details of what debt you want to be transferred.

4. The new card company will then contact your old card company about accepting the debt of your account.

5. Work with a plan to cover the debts on your new card.

The best plan is to pay more than the minimum payment.

Expect this process to take a week to complete the transfer.

Can You Transfer Other Debts to a Credit Card?

Some companies might allow you to transfer debts other than credit card debt to a new card. These include debts like monthly payments for certain fixed debts or loan charges.

The process works as the bank that provides you with a credit card could send monies to a car dealer, mortgage loan provider, or another group that requires payments from you. This measure is attractive to you help cover many debts, but you must be aware of the minimums involved each month.

The minimum payments might increase based on the debts you are transferring to a new card. The added minimums might be too high for you to handle.

Special Concerns

The process for completing a balance transfer can be easy, but you must look at a few important concepts when getting such a transfer to work for you.

- Calculate how much money you will be able to pay off before the interest rate or reduced interest period ends.

You must get as much of your debt paid so you will not spend too much on interest charges.

- Be aware of the length of time you will be able to take advantage of a free or low-interest rate on the new card.

The interest rate on the balance you transfer onto a new card might be lower than the regular or posted rate of that card. Sometimes the transfer rate will revert to the regular rate before you get enough of your debt paid off.

- Be aware of how the payments on your transfer are allocated.

The allocation of payments on your card is important to understand. Sometimes the credit card company will cover the new purchases you have made first. In other cases, the money you transferred onto the card will be paid off first. Review the terms of your new card.

- Don't ever assume that you can get a second transfer to your new card.

A credit card company might limit you to activating only one transfer on a card in its lifetime. It is clearly best to avoid getting into the same habits that caused you to require the balance transfer to begin with, but you should still make note of what is allowed.

Be cautious if you wish to use a balance transfer to repair your credit. A transfer can help you with keeping your expenses from being a threat.

Chapter 28 – Minimum Payments on Your Credit Cards

When you get your credit card bill, you will notice that you can make a minimum payment. The minimum payment is designed as a suggestion only to avoid being in arrears.

Naturally, it is always a good idea to pay at least the minimum payment on your debt. This is to keep you from being charged late payment fees that might do more harm to your credit profile. You should make payments well above the minimums to get the most out of your payment efforts.

The Dangers of Only Making Minimum Payments

Some people have lots of debts and cannot pay more than with minimum payments. The risks associated with minimum payments can be too great.

Only working with minimum payments on your credit cards can prove to be harmful to your credit as you are not doing a lot to pay off your debts.

On the surface, this might suggest that you could spend twenty months paying off that card that has $4000 in debt accumulated. The reality of this is that the interest charges on your card will only add up.

For instance, you might have a card with a 20% interest rate. You might pay $200 on a $4,000 debt to reduce it to $3,800. However, that 20% interest rate will only add more debt to your account. If you chose to pay $200 per month on that card, you would end up paying an extra $900 or in interest charges. It would take 25 months to pay off the card rather than 20 months that you had planned. That's five months longer than anticipated and nearly a thousand dollars more in interest.

Even worse, the principal total on your card will keep on increasing because of those added interest charges. You could have $100 or more in added to your card due to all the extra interest totals that are building up on your card.

While you might be keeping yourself from being hit by late fee charges, you are not necessarily doing yourself a favor with minimum payments. You would only be making your credit card debts harder to cover.

Now, let's say that you were to pay $400 on that card every month. Most of that payment would go directly on to the principal. You would pay off the loan much earlier than 20 months.

When is it Acceptable to Make Minimum Payments?

Although you should avoid minimum payments, there are times when you have no choice but to choose to do that. This could be in cases where you have many lines of credit to pay off at a time. Maybe the funds you have for handling your debts might be minimal.

There are many times when it would be acceptable to make the minimum payments on your credit cards. These aren't necessarily the best times for you, but you might not have a choice:

1. You might need to make minimum payments if you have lots of lines of debts that need to be covered.

2. Minimum payments are acceptable if you have not had any new lines of income within a certain time period or your income is steady.

3. You could also make those minimum payments if you are uncertain about what particular lines you should pay off first.

4. You have not added any new charges to a line of credit.

The main point to see about minimum payments is that they need to be avoided if possible. Be sure to keep the minimum payments as infrequent as possible.

Don't Forget Loans

You cannot afford to ignore loans when it comes to minimum payments. Credit cards are not the only debts that you should avoid making minimum payments on. You should also avoid making minimum payments on loans if possible.

The loans you are paying on can be very high in value, especially when it comes to your home and your car. You need to make sure those loans are paid regularly or else the interest charges and late fees will add up and your credit rating will be damaged.

You should think about making extra payments on loans if possible. This is to help you reduce the amount of interest that you would have to spend on your loan while also reducing the monthly payment charges.

You should also consider any early repayment fees on your loan. These fees or penalties might be worth a percentage of your loan. Consider if it is worthwhile for you to pay off a loan early.

Not all loans have early repayment charges or penalties. Of course, your credit rating will improve dramatically if you can pay those loans sooner.

Chapter 29 – Closing or Canceling Accounts

After you pay off a credit card, you might feel a desire to tear up the card and close out your account. Put those scissors away. Canceling those old accounts that you have paid off will only do more harm to your credit rating.

There are many reasons to keep those accounts open:

1. Your credit utilization ratio will go up when you close accounts.

The amount of credit available to you will decline when you close an account. Therefore, your credit utilization ratio will increase because you are spending less money or no money on your account.

Let's say that you have about $50,000 in credit that you can use. One of these would be a credit card with a limit of $10,000 that you just paid off after owing thousands of dollars on it. You might consider closing that credit card account, but that would cause the total amount of credit you can use to $40,000.

Now let's say that you had $8,000 in debts that you had to cover. Before you closed that account, you would have a credit utilization ratio of 16%. When the total amount that you can use declines to $40,000, you will have a credit utilization ratio of 20%. This means that you are using more money on your debts, thus making you a greater risk.

2. Your credit history will not be as long as it could be.

Remember that an older credit history with lines of credit having been held for years is always good to have. Closing off an old account will cause your credit history to become much shorter.

Getting rid of one line that is six years old could hurt if that was your oldest account. The oldest account would shorten your history.

   3. The variety of accounts you have could be reduced.

You have to show an ability to handle all your accounts at any time. By reducing the accounts you have, you might be admitting to credit reporting groups that you are incapable of making those payments. This could end up making it harder for some groups to take you seriously as you try to get your debts in control.

Therefore, the best thing that you can do is to keep that old line of credit open.

Chapter 30 – Closing a Credit Line

The decision to close down a credit line or credit card might be a tough challenge. Sometimes you have no choice but to close that line of credit.

- Your credit line might cost you to handle even if you are not going to use it.

- You have had trouble many times with that certain line of credit. This includes several cases where you have lost track of your funds.

- You no longer have a need for a certain credit line. You might move away and the line of credit is no longer useful. Perhaps you no longer do business with a company.

Some credit cards include annual fees or other maintenance charges that you would have to regularly pay.

There are a few things you can do to close a line of credit:

1. Always review the fees associated with the credit line that you are contemplating closing.

Fees might be a certain percentage of your credit line or just a fixed fee. Review the terms on your card to determine what the fees for closing the line are. Sometimes you might not have to pay closing fees.

2. Ask the card company if any costs associated with that line can be reduced.

Sometimes a creditor would be willing to reduce some of the burdens relating to a certain line. This is often done to keep people from leaving. You might be able to negotiate a deal where you can get some fees removed from your line of credit.

3. Avoid closing the oldest line of credit on your credit report.

4. Do not close many accounts all at once.

Closing all or the majority of your lines of credit could be seen as admitting a lack of responsibility. This makes the negative impact of closing just one account magnified.

5. Be extremely cautious with regards to balance transfers.

As appealing as it might be to transfer the balance on one line of credit to another, the fees involved could be high. You must be aware of the overall terms surrounding the balance transfer process when getting this plan to work for you.

Chapter 31 – Can You Open New Credit?

You might think that opening a new line of credit would be a smart idea when you consider how that would increase your available credit and by doing so it would not make an impact on your credit rating.

That does not mean that opening new lines of credit is always going to be the best thing to do.

This chapter focuses on new lines of credit.

Types of Lines of Credit

Choosing the best possible line of credit is important. In fact, many credit card companies and other groups often target people with poor credit ratings and promote cards to them. Those lines of credit are not always going to work when the risks associated with them are considered.

Here are some of the best lines of credit:

Lines With a Limited Reach

Take a look at the general reach of a line of credit. The reach refers to where that credit card can be used. You might be very limited as to where that card is accepted.

A retail credit line is noteworthy in that you're only going to be able to use the line at that retailer. This could work if you regularly shop at a certain place and you would still have to ensure the line is paid off regularly.

A good idea for a line with a limited reach is to look at how you can pay for the line. A good option to see entails having an option to pay for the line immediately after you spend money on it. For instance, you might spend something at a retail store on a charge card and then pay it off right away inside the same store.

You will find that stores are often willing to accept payments after people use their cards to make purchases. A retailer will not have to pay any credit fees for in-store charge transactions. Therefore, the retailer is already getting its money's worth from your purchase.

Lines With Smaller Limits

A small limit is often good enough to keep on the path toward managing your credit. A line of credit such as this could be used to buy fuel for your vehicles, for instance. Suppose you spend around $100 on gas every month. Having a card with a limit of $500 and using that card only for gas purchases is helpful as it lets you use the card exclusively for one thing while also having something that can be easy to cover and pay off. This will indicate that you are responsible for certain expenses.

You must keep the line as narrow and focused as possible. This is to keep you from being at risk of overspending.

Spacing Requests

You must be cautious with the timing of your credit applications in the event you choose to get new credit. Having too many applications for new credit in a brief amount of time can prove to be risky.

Those who send in lots of requests in little time will be seen as risky people to do business with. The inquiries that result on your account are not going to make a big change in your credit score.

In addition, you must watch for how some credit card groups and other credit-producing entities might decline you because they notice that your credit report has many inquiries. A creditor will have the same access to your credit report as you. Those who see that you are trying to get many lines of credit might become worried about you and will choose to not allow you credit.

The Benefits of a Credit Card

One of the main reasons why people often open new lines of credit is because they know there are benefits associated with them. You've already read about frequent flyer miles cards and cash back cards.

Although the benefits of such a card might prove to be useful, you must be aware a few things:

- Look at the rates and fees associated with the card. Sometimes a card with rewards might cost more to use.

- Review the terms associated with the rewards in question. These include terms surrounding what you need to do to earn those rewards.

- Decide if you will use those rewards. A frequent flyer mile card would only be beneficial if you regularly travel for business.

Knowing the benefits of your card is important for you to review.

Chapter 32 – The Risks of a Department Store Card

One of the things that people often do when aiming to build their credit lines involves using department store cards. Such will provide a person with the ability to spend money at just one retailer.

Many of these department store cards have special rewards. Some places give people access to exclusive sales or cash back offers among other things. Even though a department store card might be appealing and worthwhile, that does not mean it is always the best thing to have.

What's the Interest Rate?

Since a department store card cannot be used beyond that store, the card would probably have a higher interest rate. For instance, a typical credit card might have a rate of 15 to 20 percent. For a department store card, the rate could be from 20 to 30 percent. To avoid interest charges, a person would be advised to pay off the account each month.

What's the Annual Fee?

Some department stores will not charge an annual fee. This is helpful in many situations, particularly in cases where a store is only in a certain geographic part of the country. If that store has an online presence, it might have an annual fee that is the same as what you would spend on any traditional credit card.

Tips

There are a few extra tips for finding one of these cards for your credit use:

1. Think about how often you shop at the store that you are getting your card for.

Having plenty of cards on hand from different retailers might be useful to some, but that does not mean it will always work out. Applying for too many cards at a time can be dangerous when those inquiries on a credit report are considered. Not actually using those lines of credit could be a problem as it is useless to increase one's credit score.

2. Review the deadlines for paying off each of these cards.

You should be given an appropriate notice for when you need to make payments on your cards.

3. Be aware of the perks that come with a card, but make sure they are ones you know you would take advantage of.

Some of the special things that come with a card include exclusive discount offers, cashback deals, shipping offers for online orders and early access to certain sales. You should only use cards that feature deals you know you can use.

4. There might be times when a reward-based card is all that you really need.

Some retailers also focus on reward-based cards. These include cards that give you cash back rewards or discounts on a future purchase. One of these cards is not going to be useful as a charge or credit card. It is useful when you're trying to pay off a debt with cash but you still want to get some rewards from your purchase.

A good example of this entails what might happen when you have a card with a small limit for a grocery store. You might have seen cases where you can get special discounts on purchases at a store by presenting a loyalty card. This provides people with discounts and occasional rewards based on purchases. The card collects information on someone's payment information, purchasing history, demographics, and other details. The retailer would use this data to find out who shops there and what that person's demographics are. Those details will not include identifying information of the loyalty card holder.

5. Some department store cards support Visa, MasterCard, or another major credit card company. It might be best to avoid these options.

The rewards offered by one of these cards can be appealing. A reward could be a point scheme where you could earn special discounts or points to accumulate.

Those credit cards might prove to be expensive with high rates and fees involved.

Department store cards can be attractive and may provide good ways for people to get the most out of what they are doing to handle their credit, but such a card is not always going to be the right thing to have for resolving credit concerns. You would need to be cautious if you wish to use such cards.

Chapter 33 – Gardening Your Credit

An option for getting your credit managed is doing nothing special with your credit profile. You might be better off not working with any new credit line to repair your credit.

You could choose to manage the current lines you have and learn to garden your credit.

The Concept of Gardening

The main concept of gardening your credit is focusing on what you owe right now. You will not try to open new lines of credit, nor will you make any inquiries on your credit report. The key is to look at what you have at the moment and find ways to resolve issues or other concerns that might have shown up on your credit report.

To grow your credit through gardening:

- You are working to have negative items to disappear from your report or to at least be further in the past.

- You will work toward paying off the debts that you have right now. This includes working with on-time payments plus payments that are more than the minimums.

- You might also wait for your accounts to age so the history part of your report will improve.

Create a Timeframe

Make a plan for your goals to pay off your lines of credit that includes the following:

1. Decide on a goal to manage your current lines of credit.

2. Set a date to accomplish that goal.

Always be realistic when setting a date. A few months would be realistic.

3. Follow goals to ensure there are no problems with your credit.

Ideas to Garden Your Credit

Let's look at some of the things that you can do to garden your existing credit:

1. Check on the payment dates of your debts.

You can consider creating new payment dates for the debts you have if you feel they might be too hard to manage. By changing those dates, it becomes easier for you to make payments on-time, thus reducing the chance of incurring late fees. Be advised that not all of your payments can be managed within certain dates.

2. Prepare payment alerts relating to those dates.

3. Plan and contribute to an emergency savings account.

4. Attempt to have the creditors change the rates on your debts if possible.

Perhaps you have improved upon your credit rating over time. In this case, you might consider getting some of the loans or other debts that you have reorganized.

The general point about gardening your credit is to make it easier for you to handle your credit lines.

Chapter 34 – The Debt Snowball

The debt snowball is paying off the smallest credit card balances that you have first and then move forward.

The best part of following the debt snowball strategy is that it helps you to keep your debts in check by ensuring that the number of creditors you have will be progressively reduced over time.

You need to consider how much time it will take for you to get your payments covered.

Can This Work for Any Expense?

The debt snowball strategy is typically considered for credit card bills. That doesn't mean you have to focus exclusively on those debts. You can use the debt snowball strategy on all of the debts you have, including not only credit card debts but also loan debts and other bills.

You don't necessarily have to incorporate your home expenses. The home mortgage loan is too high in value to work for the snowball process. Just completing the snowball process helps you to improve upon how well you can handle other expenses in your life.

When to Start

As useful as the debt snowball strategy can be, it is important for you to only start the snowball move when you have the money on hand. To start, you need to be current on your bills before you can get the snowball to start working for you.

You must also have a backup fund on hand. This gives you an emergency fund to use in the event that you need extra cash while working with the debt snowball strategy. This backup fund will be discussed later.

The Process

1. Make a list of all your debts.

As mentioned earlier, you do not need to list your mortgage loan debt at this stage.

You can consider debts such as medical bills and credit card debts.

2. Make minimum payments on all of those debts with the exception of the smallest debt.

The minimum payments are needed to simply keep you from adding more interest charges or late fees.

3. Pay as much as you can on your smallest debt as possible.

Always go as well above your minimum payment. The snowball payment method is designed to have those lower-valued debts paid in full as soon as possible.

4. After you get the smallest debt paid off, move on to the next smallest debt. Repeat the process.

5. Keep moving along with the debt snowball until all your debts have been paid off in full.

The process will vary in length based on how much you owe. This process is not going to be too hard to manage provided you know what debts you need to pay off first and you have a sensible plan to pay off everything.

How Much Should Your Payments Be?

One idea to consider for managing your payments on the debt snowball is to determine how much you owe on each of the items you are trying to pay off. The following strategy may work in this situation:

1. Look at the minimum payments of each of the accounts you are trying to pay off.

2. Add the total value of those minimum payments.

3. Review the minimum payment of your lowest debt. Decide on a higher payment for that debt.

4. Keep the payment total for all those debts the same as you go through the debt snowball. This is regardless of how many debts you have left.

Keeping the same debt payment each month is a good idea as this gives you a bit of control over how you're managing your debts. For instance, the total values of the minimum payments you might make could total $650. You could consider making a payment of $50 more than the minimum for the smallest debt that you have. You would pay $700 for those payments.

After you clear out that first debt, you would still have a $700 monthly payment. You would increase the minimum payment on the new lowest debt to reflect the $700 that you will spend on your debts each month. This helps you to keep consistency in making your payments, paying off those debts sooner, and keeping interest charges from accruing.

How Long Should the Snowball Last?

There are no limits as to how much time you should spend using the debt snowball. Your best bet is to set a certain timeframe for your payments.

Let's say that you owe $7,000 in debt. You might set a timeframe of 18 months. Now, let's suppose the total value of the minimum payments of all your debts is $500. You could consider making minimum payments totaling $600 on your debts. Assuming that the totals increase to $8,000 when interest charges are considered, you could get everything paid off in 14 months. If you increased the payments to $800 per month you would get it all paid in 10 months. This ensures you are covering those debts much faster while possibly saving a few hundred dollars in added debt charges.

You should only pay off the total at a rate that is comfortable for you.

When Is This Appropriate?

The debt snowball can work best if you have multiple debts that are worth thousands of dollars. The snowball is useful if you need to cover debts with a total of $1,000 or less per month. You could still spend more money each month on the debt snowball provided that you have enough money to cover this.

You must use the debt snowball when you know you will not add anything to the debts you are trying to pay off. For instance, you might use this for student debts, car loans, medical bills, and for credit cards that you will not add charges.

Momentum Is the Key

The important thing about the debt snowball is that it is designed to provide you with the momentum you need to retire all the debts you have accumulated. As those charges are reduced and you keep the snowball under control, it becomes easier for you to get those debts managed.

You will feel confident in your ability to get all of your debts paid off. The decrease in your debt obligations will show that you are putting in a conscious effort.

You should look at how well the debt snowball can work for you if you keep the momentum and not lose sight of your ultimate goal – being debt-free.

Chapter 35 – The Reverse Snowball

You can also use the reverse snowball option to manage your balances. A better way to explain the reverse snowball is that it is like an avalanche. That is, the highest debt is paid off first while the smallest debts will be covered over time.

The highest charges are not necessarily going to be your largest debt. You may also use the reverse snowball to cover the debts that have the highest interest rates.

You still have the option to focus on the debts with the highest balances first if you wish. You could still reduce the interest charges associated with those debts. This is all up to you.

The process of the reverse snowball is:

1. List and review the debts that you have. Like with the snowball effect, you must not include a mortgage debt.

2. Review both the interest rates of each of those debts and the balances owed on each debt.

3. After choosing which option you wish to use, organize those debts by paying the minimums for the smaller ones and as far above the minimum as possible on the largest debt or the debt that has the greatest interest rate.

The goal is to cut down on the interest charges involved in the most expensive payment. The cutback on the interest should reduce the burden you have on some debts.

4. After the most expensive debt is no longer the most expensive, you can choose to either keep paying the minimum for that debt or you can start working to reduce a different debt.

Whatever the case may be, you must still pay more than the minimum on at least one of those payments.

When Should This Strategy be Used?

The reverse snowball may work when you are dealing with credit cards that have extremely high interest rates. This strategy can also be useful if you don't have lots of debts. It may be easier for you to use the reverse snowball because without the strategy it would take longer to pay off the largest debt.

Chapter 36 – An Emergency Bank Account

Having the money on hand for covering your debts is always important. However, you should not ignore other expenses in your life. The last thing you want to do when repairing your credit and managing your debts is to ignore other things that are important.

Having an emergency bank account ready for your use is vital to ensure that you can continue to keep all your regular debts paid while you are managing the other debts that have built up over time.

The emergency account would be used to pay unexpected expenses. This is a preventative measure to prevent debts from becoming delinquent.

1. Start by choosing a bank or credit union to open an account.

Sometimes the bank or union you are already with would be happy to help you start up a new account in your name. You should consider how accessible your money will be and what the overdraft penalties might be. Interest rates will be negligible.

Find out if the account has minimums. The minimum should be a few hundred dollars in value.

2. Decide how you will use your account.

You have to use this new account for issues like someone being injured and having to go to the hospital or car issues that occur. You can also use this to manage regular utility payments or other small expenses.

3. Deposit the appropriate amount of money into your account.

You should try to deposit at least $1,000 to this account. This should be enough for managing any sudden expenses. You could consider adding extra every once in a while but try to maintain a balance of at least $1,000. There are no limits to how much money you should have in your account.

4. Be sure you plan a schedule for how that emergency account is to be used.

The schedule for your account can include anything relating to expenses including utility payments, regular deposits into that account, and so forth.

Chapter 37 – Consolidating Loans

One of the most popular options you can consider for debt relief and credit repair is consolidating loans. This is suitable if you have many loans that are difficult to maintain. This could also be used if you have many credit card debts or other lines of credit that have interest being charged. All of those unsecured debts could be consolidated into one account, thus giving you the ability to manage payments easier.

1. Many of the loans that you have will be combined into one large loan.

2. The group that you use to consolidate your loans and debts will consult the creditors individually get have their balances transferred.

3. You will then be subject to a certain interest rate for that new loan. The rate will vary based on the financial company or bank.

4. You would then be required make regular monthly payments on that loan. The payments will include principal and interest. These payments should be made at the same time every month. This is much easier to manage than trying to pay on several loans at the same time.

The good thing about this is that many lenders are willing to agree to a loan consolidation. Those lenders recognize your attempt to get your debts under control. They are only too happy to do so because they benefit from the interest charges.

What is the New Interest Rate?

In many cases, the new interest rate will be a few percentage points below what you might have spent in the past.

How is that interest rate determined?

1. The interest rates on all the loans being consolidated are considered.

2. The rates are added together and the average is calculated.

3. The average interest rate will be rounded up to the nearest whole percentage point or the nearest tenth or eighth of a point.

This process can work to give you a sensible rate, but you must consider the rate before you sign for the loan. Make sure it is reasonable and fair.

You will have a significantly easier time covering your debts with a consolidated loan. You only have one payment to make each month, not to mention reduced risks associated with late fees.

The Risks of Consolidation

On the surface, consolidation sounds like an appealing solution for your debt relief and credit repair. However, consolidation is still a risky endeavor. There are a few problems associated with the consolidation that must be noticed:

1. Not all creditors are willing to accept consolidation.

Sometimes a group might refuse to work with a consolidation plan. American Express has been known to be extremely stubborn when it comes to consolidation, for instance. Therefore, no one should assume that every debt that one has could be accepted in the same consolidation plan.

2. Not all types of debts will qualify for a consolidation loan.

Sometimes an expense might be too large. For instance, a mortgage loan will clearly not qualify for consolidation because that loan is too valuable and dependent on other things. A car loan may not qualify for the process unless the loan is for a vehicle that is rather low in value.

3. The payment plan requires you to make payments on-time.

The late fees and penalties associated with a consolidation loan are often more than the charges of traditional loans. Anyone who cannot handle the loan would surely be in real trouble.

4. Added charges could go onto one's old account during the consolidation process.

Any added credit that goes into one's name during consolidation could prove to be difficult. These added charges would add to the balance of what one owes.

Other Points to Review

- You might be subjected to certain fees associated with the consolidation loan. These include costs to register your loan.

- The accounts associated with the loan are not going to be frozen during the process and can still be used to incur more debt, which is an undesirable situation.

- Only those with good credit ratings may qualify for some of these consolidating loans. The rules will vary according to the provider.

- The credit score an applicant has might influence the rate of the consolidation loan, but the weight that is placed on this will vary by group.

Chapter 38 – Refinancing Your Loans

Those who work hard to manage their debts would have much better credit scores. This, in turn, gives people the opportunity to arrange loans with more favorable terms.

One way how you can have a better credit rating is by getting your loans refinanced. You can ask your lender to give you a new interest rate.

1. Your credit rating would be analyzed by looking at its value now versus what it was like at the start of the loan.

2. The lender would then review how well you have been paying off the loan as it is.

3. If appropriate, the lender could then offer a new loan that would replace the old one. Specifically, the money that was owed in that old loan can be moved into something that has a lower rate and some more favorable terms. A new timeframe may also be added to the loan.

This point can be ideal for many needs. A person might be able to spend less time paying off the loan. In many cases, the payments that would be used on that loan would be dramatically lower than what was used at the start.

Refinancing is appropriate for auto loans for the most part, although a mortgage loan may also qualify for refinancing. Not all lenders are willing to offer to refinance.

The Steps to Refinance

These steps are the basics for managing the refinancing process, but the specifics of these steps may vary according to the particular group that you negotiate with.

1. Start by gathering the appropriate documents for your account.

   - Information on your loan as it is

This includes details on how much you owe on the loan, what its rate is, the term left on the loan, and how you have been making payments ready.

   - Income details including your work status

   - Your driver's license, Social Security Number, or any other identifying information

2. Check on your credit report.

You should look at your latest credit report to see that its value has increased. Be aware of any negative items on your report as well. Refer to the earlier sections of this guide to see what you can do if you need to dispute anything on your report.

3. Review the details of a proposed refinancing plan.

You have to look at the benefits of refinancing, such as:

   - What would you spend each month on your loan if you refinanced?

   - How would the term of the new loan differ?.

   - See if there are any early repayment penalties in the refinancing plan.

Look at how much you spend on interest charges and other fees. Those fees should be smaller in value than what you would have to spend on with your current loan. If they are not smaller, you can avoid the refinancing process as you would possibly spend more by refinancing.

4. When talking with a refinancing team, ask about options you might have.

You may be given the option to either reduce the rate on your loan or to stretch the length of the loan. You would be rewarded by smaller monthly payments. Determine what the current and long-term expenses would be versus what you are spending on your expenses right now.

5. After agreeing to the refinancing process (if applicable), fill out the proper documents with the loan provider.

At this point, you should have a new loan to work with while using a better cost structure for the long run.

Is Refinancing Worthwhile?

The most important thing you can do when looking at your loan is to see if refinancing is to your financial benefit.

Let's say that you have a car loan on which you currently owe $10,000. You might have a 6.9% rate on it with 36 months left on that loan. You would be spending $308 per month on that loan at this point. This would be about $1,100 on interest versus the $10,000 that you owe.

You may be able to refinance that loan with a better interest rate. You might get a lower interest rate of 4.9%, but you would also get the loan stretched to 48 months. You would clearly get a better monthly payment of $230, but you would also pay about $1,030 in interest.

This is a good offer and would suggest that you should choose to refinance. At the same time, you could still ask to have the same 36 months to handle the payments. You would owe about $300 per month, which does not sound like much of a cut, but you would save nearly $300 on interest during the course of the refinanced loan.

Of course, sometimes the changes might be extremely minimal and would not make much of an impact. It is up to you to decide if refinancing is worthwhile.

Chapter 39 – The Risk of Using Credit Repair Companies

You might be tempted to work with credit repair companies. You might hear stories about businesses online. These companies advertise quite often online because they know there are people who might be desperate.

A credit repair group is an organization that claims to offer a service to resolve your credit issues. They claim that they can resolve the problems with your account. That does not mean that such a group would be the best to contact.

Although you might think you will help yourself when you contact a credit repair team for help, this could end up causing more problems than what you might afford to handle. This is because they would do the same things that you could easily do on your own.

What Does a Credit Repair Company Do?

A credit repair company will do many things to help you get your credit repaired. These include such things as the following:

- A team will ask for a credit report from each of the reporting bureaus.

- The negative items on your report can be reviewed to see if they can be disputed.

- A formal dispute may be sent on your behalf.

- A team may also negotiate with the bureaus to get negative items removed.

These services sound appealing enough, but they are things that you could do on your own. To make things worse, the repair company will charge you for the service and this is problematic when you consider that you can do what they provide yourself or with a minimal amount of money.

What is the Cost?

The cost imposed by one of these groups for credit repair services could be prohibitive. You could potentially spend at least $80 to $125 per month to get one of these services to work for you. It might take for a group months to review information on your account. The group might wait for a few weeks before doing anything with your information. This is to charge you for an added month or two. The repair contract could be for at least four to six months depending on the terms of the contract. Considering the hundreds of dollars you could lose in the process, this would end up being a bad choice.

An additional problem could be that you might ask for help in some form only to find out that you don't have any errors on your report to begin with. Checking on your report yourself is best as you can use this to understand what you can do next. Hiring someone to help only to find that there are no problems on a report would only be a total waste of effort and money.

The amazing thing about these debt repair companies is that they continue to stay active and profitable because so many people are gullible enough to fall for what they are offering.

Focus more on your own work to resolve your credit-related issues for four reasons:

1. You have more control over the process.

2. You will get answers to your concerns sooner.

3. It costs much less for you to have the dispute resolved on your own.

4. The processes that you have read about in this guide are not difficult to use.

While a credit repair group might have the best of intentions that does not mean that the group is going to be useful to you or likely to give you the support you need.

Chapter 40 – Managing Credit Repair If Your Identity Has Been Stolen

No one wants to think about what might happen when one's identity is stolen. It is a fact of life that all people must be aware of. There is always a chance that a person might have one's identity stolen. In fact, identity theft is a big part of why many people get into credit repair procedures. They want to do what they can to resolve their credit problems because they know their identities were used to open various accounts in their name.

The credit repair process to identity theft-related issues is not complicated.

1. Notify any banks or creditors about the identity theft.

The first thing you have to do is to inform everyone you do business with about the identity theft. This includes charges on your accounts that were not made by you.

More often than not you will not be held liable. You might be required to spend up to $50 on an unauthorized charge in accordance with the Fair Credit Billing Act.

2. Contact your credit bureaus to let them know about the fraud situation.

A fraud alert should be given to the bureaus to help with helping you to keep your credit rating from being at risk. The alert should be added for about 90 days, thus giving the authorities to investigate.

3. Review your credit reports to see what things were added as a result of the identity theft.

These may include various lines of credit that were opened by someone other than you. Check on your payment history to see if there are charges you did not approve as well as any new inquiries that were made on your account.

You also have the option to have a credit freeze on your account. A freeze will prevent anyone from accessing your credit report or using your lines of credit.

4. Prepare a letter of dispute to the credit bureaus to discuss these lines of credit.

You would have to enclose a copy of your credit report and highlight any errors that you have found on your report. This includes details on the account or accounts that you had not authorized to be opened.

5. Provide the appropriate police reports or other documents surrounding the investigation about your stolen identity.

You would have to talk with your local police when your identity has been stolen.

The key is to have as many documents as possible to support your position and your claim that your identity was stolen and used fraudulently.

6. Send your letter to the bureaus via certified mail service.

7. Talk with as many financial institutions relating to your debts as possible.

You may get help having some of these accounts closed or frozen or any collections against them stopped.

The process for managing credit repair in the event of identity theft can take some time to complete and every instance is unique.

Additional Points

There are a few extra things that should be done when you are trying to manage a situation where your identity has been stolen:

1. Change all the passwords on your accounts so no one will be at risk of breaking into those accounts.

2. Talk with the Social Security Administration about getting a proper review of your account. This could help you to keep your number from being accessible.

There are times when you might be given a new Social Security Number, but this rarely ever happens. There is a reduced likelihood that your account can be used further.

3. Apply for a new driver's license.

It is much easier for you to replace your driver's license number than it is to do the same for your SSN. You can contact your local DMV office to apply for a new license.

4. Contact any companies that you deal with regularly. This could help keep your address identity private so no one can try to access your data.

The only thing you can really do at this point is to be patient and carefully monitor activity on your accounts. Wait for the authorities to complete their investigations.

Chapter 41 – Credit Collection Scams

One of the most common ways that people can have their identities stolen and their credit histories damaged is by credit collection scams. Many people who work on credit repair practices are often victims of such scams. These people might fall for those scams in the middle of the credit repair process. Such a problem can quickly derail one's ability to pay off the difficult debts one has.

These scams often take place online, but it is often easier to run into them through the phone. It is easy for scammers to contact someone over the phone about certain debts.

Some people might be more susceptible to these scams because they are so worried about paying off their debts and might become persuaded to pay them off prematurely.

Signs of a Scam

The most common signs of a credit collection scam include the following:

- A collector refuses to provide specific information on what the debts are for. This includes information about the original creditor.

- Payments are being requested over the phone. The scammers ask for payments to be only online or by mail.

- A collector will not give information on the agency that they claim to represent. Details on the group's phone number, address, website, or other details are not revealed.

- People who ask for specific details like a license number, credit card number, or government-issued numbers are surely a scammer. Real creditors are not going to ask for these details on the phone.

These are clear signs that show that something is wrong with a collection process, but not everyone heeds these indicators. Some will continue to assume that these collection efforts are legitimate and are willing to provide their personal data to those groups, thus giving the scammers the information to steal their identity and open new credit cards in the victim's name. By knowing the signs of a scam, you can prevent becoming a victim of one of these dangerous scammers.

What to Do If You Suspect a Scam

There are a few things that can be done if you suspect a scam is being perpetrated.

1. Find as much information about the suspected collector as possible.

Collect information, such as the phone number that the person is using to contact you, emails that someone uses, the name that person is using, and the company he says he represents.

2. Contact the original creditor.

Ask the creditor about the suspected collector. You need to confirm that the collector is known by the creditor.

3. Record any calls and keep copies of emails that you get from the collector.

4. Do not respond to the suspected collector.

5. Send a complaint to the Consumer Financial Protection Bureau regarding the situation.

Let the CFPB know as many details about the situation as possible so a proper investigation and action can be taken. You can visit consumerfinance.gov to get the help you need.

Chapter 42 – When to Sell Items To Improve Your Credit

There are often times when you might consider selling items to reduce your debt. For example, you might have an expensive vehicle and you are struggling to pay off the debt. As a result, you might sell the car and use that money to pay off a sizable portion of your debt.

The first thing to do is to consider the time it would take for you to pay off the debt. For instance, you might consider the car that you financed. Suppose you have $7,000 owing on that car and if you want to find a way to pay it off. That $7,000 debt could be paid in about two years.

You should use that two-year schedule instead of whatever your loan schedule might be. Even if your schedule entails a longer period of time, getting something paid off sooner is clearly the best thing to do when managing what you owe.

You might have to consider selling off that vehicle if you are going to take more than two years to pay it off. At this point, it could be difficult for you to afford the interest on the loan. You would have to sell the car to cover more of the charges in interest. The key is to retire that debt as soon as possible.

You are not going to lose credit points if you sell items that you owe money on. You might find that selling something you are not able to pay off might be the best thing to do so you can at least reduce the burden that you have.

The Value of the Item

The value of your item needs to be considered. You might find that its value is much less than whatever you owe on it.

When something is worth less than what is owed, that asset is officially underwater. This is not a situation that a person wants, but it can happen. A home might become less valuable due to foreclosures or the housing market is weak. A vehicle could become less valuable due to damages to that vehicle or that car having high mileage.

The best thing to do when selling something is to try and get it sold off as soon as possible. This includes getting a sale managed before the value declines any further. Anything that is held for far too long will more than likely lose its value. It is just a matter of use and aging that can cause things to become less valuable, so look carefully at what is happening when getting something sent off in the sale process.

Finding a Replacement

Although selling something you owe money on can be useful, you should consider a replacement. The new replacement vehicle or another item that you might need would require money. The best thing to do is to find something that has a cheaper value than what your loan was. Just having something cheaper and affordable might be good enough.

If you don't need to furnish a replacement, you might be decreasing your assets, but you are at least reducing your debt burden.

Chapter 43 – A New Credit File

Let's talk about how to establish another person's credit for the first time.

Even those who have existing credit lines can benefit. Maybe you might be trying to resolve your credit-related issues by linking to another person's new credit account. This could include establishing an account for your child. For instance, your child could be eighteen years of age and able to apply for credit services. You can make a joint account so you have control over the credit functions.

This could help you grow your credit as you can show that you not only care about your credit but also the credit of another person who is trying to establish an account.

The First Credit Score

A few keys should be noticed when getting a credit score for the first time. These include the following aspects for one's work:

1. A person's general ability to manage credit at the beginning of one's credit history should be reviewed.

2. The types of financial instruments being used will play a part in determining one's credit score.

These financial instruments can be low-value cards or small loans.

3. An ability to keep one's identity from being exposed.

Do not instigate several inquiries for credit. Asking for too much credit could prove to be dangerous in some cases.

Tips For Managing a New Account

A discussion is necessary between the owners of a joint account or if contemplating co-signing for a loan.

1. Agree on the use of the new account.

It should be agreed how the new credit is used and to use it only when necessary.

2. A payment schedule should also be planned.

3. Review how much money is being spent monthly or weekly.

Terms

Bankruptcy

Bankruptcy occurs when you are legally relieved of the debts that you owe. This would have to be authorized by a United States bankruptcy court.

Charge-off

When the balance on your credit debt is no longer expected to be paid off, the creditor will report that as a charge-off. This means the creditor does not anticipate that you will pay that debt. This would create substantial damage to your credit rating.

Creditor

A creditor is a party that underwrote the loan.

Debtor

A debtor is a person to whom the creditor financed a loan.

Delinquent

When your credit report lists that a payment is delinquent, that means it is late. The delinquency may be reported in 30-day increments as many collection groups adjust their charges monthly.

Inquiry

An inquiry on your account refers to when someone investigates your credit report with the intention of establishing a loan to the credit report holder.

Installment Debt

An installment debt has specific payment periods. In most cases, this requires a person to make a set payment at a particular point in the month. Mortgage and auto loans are the most prominent installment debts.

Judgment

A judgment occurs when a creditor attempts to collect money from a debtor through the courts. This may result in the court requiring a person's wages to be garnished (sent directly or to the creditor).

Lien

A lien is a secured loan. The most common liens are a mortgage or auto loan. Tax liens may also be added to one's profile in cases where a person owes unpaid taxes.

Revolving Debt

Revolving debt is different from installment debt as it involves payments that can have varying values. Credit card debt is the most commonly used form of revolving debt. The amount that is owed each month may vary, but the debtor must at least the minimum amount specified by the creditor.

Settlement

A settlement is a contract between the creditor and debtor. The two parties may settle with one another to ensure that the debt issues one has been resolved without going through a trial. A creditor may settle to collect less money from a debtor than what that person owes, but this would end up penalizing that debtor due to the inability to pay the debt in full.

Conclusion

There are many things in life that can lead to a person having an inability to manage one's credit. These problems can be dangerous and harmful. This includes problems where a person might have a general inability to pay debts or when unfortunate things happen in life that make it more difficult for people to get their credit under control.

You do not have to struggle with a poor credit rating forever. You can get the problems that are reported on your credit report to be eliminated if you put in the right effort into getting such problems under control.

The points you have read about in this guide will help you resolve debt-related issues you might have encountered. By following the suggestions in this guide, you can keep your debts under control.

Be aware of what is happening with your credit profile as you work toward repairing your credit.

Consider how you are managing your debt. Learn how certain disputes can be managed. You might be surprised how some of the legal concepts can be used to manage your debts.

Good luck with all of your efforts for managing your credit and managing your money.

www.ingramcontent.com/pod-product-compliance
Lightning Source LLC
Chambersburg PA
CBHW071603210326
41597CB00019B/3386